International Oil Policy

International Oil Policy

Foreword by Senator Edward M. Kennedy

Arnold E. Safer

LexingtonBooks
D.C. Heath and Company
Lexington, Massachusetts
Toronto

Library of Congress Cataloging in Publication Data

Safer, Arnold E
    International oil policy.

    Includes index.
    1. Energy policy—United States.   2.   Petroleum industry and trade—
Finance.   I.   Title.
HD9502.U52S23   333.8'2   79-7185
ISBN 0-669-02959-9

Published simultaneously in Canada

Printed in the United States of America

International Standard Book Number: 0-669-02959-9

Library of Congress Catalog Card Number: 79-7185

Contents

Contents

List of Figures

List of Tables

Foreword

American energy policy since 1973 has been based on the assumption that a serious shortage in world oil supply is imminent. There is no point in confronting OPEC, according to a corollary of this assumption, because OPEC is actually doing the United States and other oil-consuming nations a favor—it is forcing us to prepare now for the permanent scarcity of oil that the world will be facing in the future. According to this view, OPEC price increases merely hasten the day when high-cost alternative energy sources, especially synthetic fuels, will become commercially competitive with oil.

This "scarcity" assumption has had a paralyzing effect on American energy policy. The view that high OPEC prices are inevitable has rarely been challenged. The prospect that large untapped oil and gas resources may exist outside the OPEC nations has been almost completely ignored. Also ignored has been the stabilizing influence that the international oil companies continue to provide for the OPEC cartel. Not long ago, an imaginative plan to require the OPEC nations to bid for access to the U.S. market was dismissed by the Secretary of Energy with the question, "Do we dare?"

In 1978, the Energy Subcommittee of the Congressional Joint Economic Committee began to explore the questions surrounding the world's future oil supply and the implications for the United States. Subcommittee hearings brought together a number of witnesses who challenged the prevailing scarcity assumption. Officials of the U.S. Geological Survey testified that the world's supply of recoverable oil might well be two or three times larger than previous estimates had suggested. They also found it likely, contrary to the prevailing view, that the production costs of these new sources of oil would be well below the prices set by OPEC and also well below the marginal cost of U.S. production. The implications of this new and more optimistic view of the world's oil supply were set out for the subcommittee in excellent testimony by Dr. Arnold Safer. Dr. Safer has now expanded his views into this new and challenging book.

There is much in this volume that is controversial. There are some views I do not share. For example, I do not agree with Dr. Safer's optimism about our potential domestic oil and gas supplies. Therefore, I doubt that higher domestic prices—achieved by ending federal price controls—will lead to enough new supplies to outweigh the heavy costs imposed on consumers because of higher prices.

In his analysis of the world petroleum market, however, Dr. Safer makes an important contribution. He persuasively argues that the consuming nations need not remain passive victims of rising OPEC prices. He proposes a broad and innovative agenda for America's national and international energy policy that deserves serious study.

Like a number of petroleum experts, Dr. Safer believes that the integrated structure of the international oil industry enhances OPEC's power. OPEC's control over world oil prices would be significantly reduced if the producing nations had to sell their oil to the world's refining industry in arms length transactions, rather than through the existing noncompetitive structure of the international oil companies. Dr. Safer would have the federal government play a greater role in the world oil market, even to the point of directly involving the government in negotiating purchases of foreign oil. Ultimately, Dr. Safer would like to see the development of an international futures market for both crude oil and refined products. Such a market would substantially restrict the OPEC cartel's power to control prices in the world market.

Important as it is to stimulate competition among purchasers from OPEC, priority must also be given to another major proposal by Dr. Safer—encouraging exploration for oil and development of oil resources in non–OPEC countries.

Possibly, the prevailing current view may be correct and the world may now be nearing the end of its oil supply. But we do not know that. In fact, there are reasons to be profoundly skeptical about such assumptions. Major recent discoveries in Canada and Mexico cast serious doubt on the views of those who claim to know the limits of world supply. More oil wells have been drilled in the state of Arkansas than in all of Latin America. OPEC's hold on world supply is undoubtedly strengthened by institutional constraints on oil and gas development elsewhere in the world. Yet the United States has done little to probe the nature of these constraints. We have done even less to devise strategies for overcoming them.

A major aspect of America's energy policy must be the development of programs to encourage the diversification and expansion of world oil supply. As Dr. Safer points out, such programs will be entirely compatible with the goals of other nations. For the most part, it is likely that any new oil pools will be discovered in the poorer nations, which have suffered the most serious economic set-backs as a result of spiraling oil prices. Discovery of even small amounts of oil and gas in their territory would bring enormous benefits to such nations.

There are limits to what the United States can do. We cannot dictate the energy policies of other nations. But we can assist those who want our help to discover and develop their oil and gas potential. Our policy of promoting diversification of oil supplies must be flexible. Simple solutions are unlikely for the institutional constraints on world oil supply, but we can at least develop a range of policies. In some areas, private companies may be welcome, and a policy of encouraging private action may be sufficient. In others, government-to-government assistance may be the key to development of new resources. In still others, multilateral international arrangements may hold the answer.

Dr. Safer's most important contribution in this book is to refocus the energy debate. He has brought attention back to the most significant and most neglected energy problem—the power of OPEC over the price and supply of world oil. There will be disagreement over the specifics of the proposals in this book. But the importance of oil supply diversification and proliferation in the development of national energy policy cannot be overstated.

Senator Edward M. Kennedy
Chairman, Energy Subcommittee
of the Congressional Joint
Economic Committee

Preface

In the autumn of 1978 just hours before adjournment, a divided Congress passed a National Energy Plan by the thinnest of margins. Debate had been heated during the prior eighteen months; despite strong opposition, however, the Carter administration prevailed. While political considerations obviously played a role in the reluctance of some senators and congressmen to vote for the bill, much of the opposition may have also been caused by the nature of the proposals themselves. Real-world events over the prior eighteen months, since the president first unveiled his energy proposals, suggest that much of the program is at best irrelevant to the central trends of energy consumption and production. First, the National Energy Plan as passed by the Congress totally avoided the problem of oil, our single most important fuel whose price remains controlled by a cartel of foreign producing nations. Because of the divisiveness of the issue, Congress was unable to change the existing system of domestic oil pricing and the heavy burden of regulation that is imposed upon oil-producing companies in the United States. Second, the legislation regarding utility-rate reform, the increased use of coal, and the conservation of oil and gas will make only marginal changes in a process that the private sector is already pursuing with few directives from Washington. This includes natural gas, although on balance, I believe that the gas pricing compromise will ultimately benefit both the industry and the public.

The single most important piece of legislation in the energy conservation area was passed before Mr. Carter took office and with little or no involvement by the executive branch. This was a mandate by the Congress to the automobile industry to gradually increase the mileage efficiency of its new cars to an average of 27.5 miles per gallon by 1985. As a result, gasoline consumption in the United States, which grew historically at about 4 percent per year, is now leveling off and will be declining by 1985. Aside from this legislation, the major impact of federal involvement in the petroleum area has been negative. In particular, much of the existing legislation and its subsequent implementation have so distorted historical distribution patterns that oil imports are encouraged and domestic production is discouraged.

The congressional debate and the substantially weakened energy legislation that followed reflects the fact that our domestic energy problems do not permit both a politically acceptable and comprehensive package of solutions. The conflicts are too numerous because the political constituencies are too divided—consumer versus producer, Easterner versus Westerner, government versus business, environmentalist versus traditionalist, and low–growth conservationist versus rapid–growth labor leader. Energy issues affect almost all of our economic and social problems, from agriculture to tranportation, from welfare reform to tax reform, from urban decay to rural poverty, and from inflation to unemployment. Rational solutions to the domestic energy crisis cannot be framed to solve all of society's ills; in fact, some energy policies could exacerbate problems in some other areas. Priorities must be set, and the political rhetoric of comprehensiveness must be put aside to accommodate the political reality of compromise. As the energy bill demonstrated, that very process of compromise does not permit comprehensive or totally rational answers, at least at the present time.

On the other hand, I believe that significant progress can be made on international energy problems. There is no substantial constituency arguing in favor of oil prices dictated by the Organization of Petroleum Exporting Countries (OPEC), and the most serious flaw, both political and economic, in the president's energy package is its virtual silence about OPEC. If the president is asking the American people for sacrifices, then he should be prepared to tell them what plans he might have for attempting to dilute the price–setting powers of the cartel. Present sacrifice should have the prospect of future reward.

The administration is telling us that the world as a whole faces a physical shortage of oil by 1985 or 1990. That proposition is open to question. Oil may be scarce in the United States, at least temporarily, but it is questionable that the world as a whole is facing the prospect of a long–term shortage. By the end of 1978 OPEC had excess capacity of 10 million barrels daily, some 20 percent of world consumption. That is only in terms of proven reserves. According to even the most conservative geologists ultimately recoverable oil reserves around the world are vastly in excess of what the world will need for many decades to come. Pricing and politics, in addition to very long production lead times, are what make the difference between scarcity and abundance.

In other words, are soaring energy costs the result of an impending physical shortage or of OPEC's monopolistic–pricing practices? The answer is probably a combination of both; until the second problem is recognized, solutions to the first may be costly and ineffective.

What the president may be saying (though he may not want to say it, for fear of offending certain key oil–producing nations) is that if we conserve energy now and are able to hold down our oil imports, then in ten or fifteen years we may be able to counter the cartel. But there is something inherently contradictory in this philosophy. If there is as serious a world physical shortage as his advisors suggest, then in ten or fifteen years the United States may be so weakened politically and economically that it may not be able to respond effectively to the cartel. On the other hand, if it is only the United States that has a temporary physical shortage, then there should be something we can do today to change the mechanism by which we import our oil, and thereby at least try to obtain better commercial terms for our oil imports.

President Carter should instruct his energy-policy team to come up with an approach for dealing with OPEC now, not only in terms of oil but also in terms of the petrodollar problem that is contributing to the present worldwide economic stagnation. Today, financial and economic variables are so linked with the energy problem that policies for dealing with each separately will not work. They have in fact proved counterproductive.

This book proposes an alternative to our acceptance of the OPEC oil monopoly. By promoting the idea of an impending world scarcity of oil, the U.S. government has become unwilling to take any steps to dilute some of OPEC price-setting powers. Every consumer of oil, from large industrial users to purchasers of gasoline or heating oil, must now pay the price dictated by this foreign cartel. But there is no shortage of oil in the world, nor is there likely to be for many decades to come. Although we will have to import large quantities of oil for many years to come, we can learn to buy it better. If the government of the United States were to adopt the suggestions in this book, rising oil prices could be contained. To the extent that the prices of other energy sources (gas, coal, and so forth) are related to international oil prices, responding to the oil monopoly directly would benefit all energy users. Finally, the world's economies would improve because we would all have a little more to spend on non-oil goods and services and thereby expand employment, production, and world trade.

Acknowledgments

As a practicing economist for the past eighteen years, I have written my share of academic papers and business reports. I had neither the inclination nor the time to write a whole book. Nevertheless, after witnessing the chaos in U.S. energy policy since the disruptions of 1973, I became convinced that integrating my concepts into a book might add to public understanding of at least the international oil aspects of the energy problems facing our country. Although my ideas are both controversial and contrary to mainstream thinking in this area, many people on both sides of the political spectrum have shown interest in my project. Both liberals and conservatives will find much to praise and to criticize in this document. To my friends on both sides of the political spectrum, I say: "It is the closest I can come to the truth of the matter."

My secretary, Miss Elaine Doody, and my research assistant, Mrs. Victoria Tuason, have borne up nobly in the task of writing, rewriting, and editing. I thank them both for their patience and efforts. Most of all, I must thank my wife, Roberta, without whose prodding and encouragement this book would certainly never have come about.

International Oil Policy

1 Cry Scarcity: The False Assumption of Policy

The psychology of scarcity causes that very shortage to come about; for example, Alaskan and North Sea oil are not being produced to the maximum extent possible. Projections of future oil shortages are like a receding horizon: no matter how rapidly you move toward it, it is still the same distance away. But the very rise in world oil prices will lead to the opposite, an abundance of oil in the years ahead.

Ever since the Organization of Petroleum Exporting Countries (OPEC) cartel burst onto the scene several years ago, the notion of an impending worldwide energy shortage has become an ever more frequent theme of government, academia, and the business elite. In my opinion the scarcity thesis, first created by the intellectual apologists of OPEC, is misguided and detrimental to Western economic and political objectives. In a massive attempt to sell energy conservation to a supposedly gluttonous industrial society, government policymakers continue to advance the theory of impending world scarcity and ever higher world energy prices. They seem to neglect, however, the associated corollaries of sluggish economic growth and high inflation.

A true physical scarcity of energy supplies could occur only if the governments of the world caused it. Political impediments may very well deter—they are certainly delaying—the search for oil and gas. Yet as long as nature's hydrocarbon bounty is there to be uncovered, world governments will be unable to stop the massive treasure hunt. As long as OPEC maintains monopolistic control over world energy prices, both private and public capital will continue to flow into the development of energy resources, since potential returns will be high enough to justify continued exploration for oil and gas. At OPEC-dictated prices, finding new sources of oil and gas is the best game in town.

This is not to say that conservation and alternative energy sources are not needed. Conservation makes sense because it stresses economic efficiency. Investment in alternative fuels is necessary because it gives us a greater degree of energy self-reliance and protection from unreliable and monopoly-priced OPEC oil. These worthy goals, therefore, need not be linked to an impending world energy scarcity. The political effect of the scarcity forecast impedes us from taking the steps that would dilute some of

1

the price-setting powers of OPEC and from reaching a healthier accommodation with the legitimate aspirations of its member governments.

The Psychology of Scarcity

Let us take a closer look at where this scarcity psychology is leading energy policymakers, both here and abroad. British policymakers now talk of "husbanding their resources," in other words, stretching out North Sea oil production so that the British resource becomes more valuable as world supplies become less plentiful in the mid to late 1980s. This means *not* selling valuable oil in the surplus northern European market in the early 1980s. Under market-sensitive British oil policy, energy conservation mandates not only lowering consumption but reducing production. Thinking scarcity breeds scarcity.

In the United States the perception that we are running out of oil and gas has led to continued price controls and to such contorted schemes as the proposed crude-oil equalization tax. The domestic policy argument of the scarcity theorists seems to run as follows: If we are running out of oil, why give private industry the windfall profits obtained from higher international energy prices? If we must conserve, let us tax this price-inelastic commodity in the hope of reducing consumption.

Somewhat higher prices for new oil and gas are allowed in this scenario, but where are domestic oil companies going to get the cash flow to keep looking for the big fields? Yes, OPEC is a distortion of the international market, but why penalize U.S. companies? What is stopping us from giving them every incentive to explore and develop new reserves of domestic oil and gas? The psychology of scarcity.

The problem of Alaskan oil is another example of how policy is distorted by cries of world oil scarcity. Congressional approval of the construction of the Alaskan oil pipeline was predicated on the requirement that the oil would have to be consumed in the United States. Because of a surplus of oil on the West Coast and a lack of economic transportation to other parts of the United States, the companies would like to export a portion of the Alaskan oil to Japan. Under a temporary agreement with Japan, these oil shipments would gradually be reduced as the West Coast surplus diminished, or as lower-cost U.S. transportation alternatives became available. Otherwise the oil will simply not be produced, further limiting world supplies. Congressional fears of a growing world oil scarcity are in fact helping that very scarcity come about.

The Washington perspective on energy has focused increasingly on the proposition that the United States will soon run out of oil. To quote one former government official, "The central reality is that the end of our petroleum is in sight and, in all likelihood, the biggest oil fields have already been found. Higher prices to producers (through decontrol) will result, at best, in only marginal increases in output."[1] But this point of view is open to serious challenge, on both geological and economic grounds.

Even the most conservative geological surveys rebut the thesis that the United States will physically run out of oil in the near future. At the minimum, potential new U.S. oil reserves have been estimated at 120 billion to 150 billion barrels—at current consumption rates, seventeen to twenty years of future supply. The potential is there. What is needed to tap it is an energy policy that encourages the search for and development of new reserves.

Unfortunately, in the United States drilling for new oil has not always been encouraged. U.S. oil production has been declining since 1971 primarily because the large reserves of Alaskan oil discovered in 1968 could not be produced until a transportation system was built. Technically, a pipeline could have been put into operation within two or three years after the reserves were identified. Environmental disputes among other things, however, delayed the project. Finally, some six years later, Alaskan oil is flowing but not to the greatest possible extent. By the early 1980s U.S. oil production could well be back to the level achieved in the early 1970s, if a maximum supply policy were adopted.

Such delays in bringing on new energy supplies, coupled with government-mandated use of oil (particularly low–sulfur oil) in lieu of other fuels, brought about substantial increase in U.S. oil imports in the late 1960s and early 1970s. For a time, the historical oil import quota system kept some semblance of order in international markets. By 1972, however, the old quota system had become so full of special exemptions that it was eliminated, and the way was paved for OPEC dominance of the world's oil markets.

U.S. policy is now faced with a situation in which past regulatory excesses can be corrected only gradually. We cannot avoid paying OPEC's monopoly prices, at least until we can find and develop the significant new energy sources that geologists tell us are there.

There has been substantial debate in the past few years concerning the response of oil output to increased prices. Although all supply elasticity studies are subject to many technical and economic uncertainties, there is sufficient evidence to suggest that higher oil prices will eventually yield major increases in U.S. oil production. Figure 1-1 shows a reasonable approximation to a long–run U.S. oil supply curve. It is based on a technical assessment of each major producing area in the United States and is adapted from studies done in 1971 and 1972 by the National Petroleum Council.[2] The suggested production levels along the horizontal axis consist of first–year output derived from newly discovered reserves, assumed to be produced over a fifteen-year period. All secondary and tertiary costs and

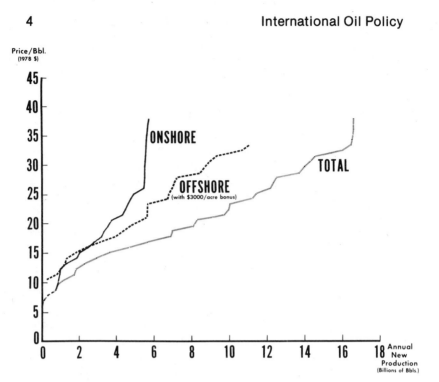

Source: Adapted from 1971 National Petroleum Council Estimates
Figure 1-1. Incremental Oil Supply Curve (United States)

potential production are excluded. A 10 percent cost of capital is assumed. There is no attempt to account for the timing of the investments needed to create the new oil reserves nor to delineate when the production from the reserves would come on-stream. It does provide, however, a reasonable estimate of potential production rates that could be attained at various prices.

The principal point of figure 1-1 is that higher oil prices will induce more oil production from newly discovered oil fields. For example, a price of about $15 for wellhead crude oil in the United States would eventually bring about an increase of 5.5 billion barrels of annual new production. This is equivalent to 15 million barrels per day (MMB/D), or 75 percent of current U.S. oil consumption. Other studies suggest that the secondary and tertiary recovery techniques can eventually increase current oil production by 30 percent to 40 percent, or an additional annual output of 3 MMB/D, provided that the higher prices suggested here can be obtained to justify the extra investment expenditures.

We may, as some contend, run out of oil, but this is not an immediate possibility. Economic studies show that as of now U.S. oil production could be significantly increased if prices were permitted to rise to reflect market forces. Geologic studies show that the reserves are there.

The key question is whether government policy should be guided primarily by the current long-range "official" forecasts of worldwide scarcity. I make forecasts for decision making by private companies, in which the quantity and distribution of current capital spending is partially influenced by the future outlook. That, of course, is a legitimate planning tool for private corporations, in the microeconomic sense. For government, however, it is a dubious practice. No one can tell with sufficient precision to frame national policy how much new oil will be available beyond four or five years—exploration may identify vast new resources or it may come up dry. It is current or near-term exploration that will identify what is available from newly discovered sources within the longer-term, ten- or fifteen-year horizon. In fact, these very long range forecasts are highly suspect. Oil company executives know this, but they also know that it is their business to make current decisions that will affect their long-run financial and operating results. They will take actions now to negate the current projections as much as possible. Can governments do this? More important, should they?

My answer is no. As I see it, governments should provide a climate in which private sector forces can act. If government policy is now turning toward a priority of maximum energy supplies, it is likely that other political constraints have become so overriding that a maximum supply policy will not, in fact, be pursued. Underlying these political constraints is the perverse conception of a looming worldwide oil shortage. Some environmentalists and those espousing the "limits to growth" hypothesis propagate the psychology of scarcity because it fits neatly into their preconceived notions of the disaster toward which the industrial world is heading. And if the crisis is coming, *they* should be appointed to stop it. Consumer advocates and labor leaders use the psychology of scarcity to keep the "fat cats" in the oil companies from getting a bigger piece of the energy pie. These same oil companies meanwhile promote the psychology of scarcity to induce the government regulatory establishment to permit higher prices. Finally, the psychology of scarcity solidifies the position of the regulators themselves, in that the impending shortage must be planned for and present supplies allocated by Washington.

The Oil Shortage As a Receding Horizon

How long will our oil last? When will we run out? Why should we use up our precious oil reserves now when a world shortage is so close at hand? All these questions, raised again and again in one form or another, reflect a basic misconception about the oil industry, or about business planning in general. Proven oil reserves represent expensive capital committed to inventories; no business chooses to tie up more capital than it has to in assets that will not yield income for many years. Thus the incentive for further exploration is in large part based on perceptions by oil company executives about the adequacy of the industry's existing reserves and their own role in the industry picture. Future oil price expectations, and therefore the motivation to expand or contract capital spending for oil exploration, are extremely sensitive to this notion of adequacy. Adequacy is not a totally physical concept; it also relates to the expected economic returns (revenues minus costs relative to investment) that existing or potential oil reserves will yield.

Figure 1-2 shows both worldwide (excluding the Communist bloc) and U.S. ratios of proven reserves to annual production from 1947 to the present. The ratio measures how many years of future supplies of proven oil reserves we have left. The key word is *proven* because figure 1-2 says nothing about how much more might be left to be found.

This R/P ratio (reserves/production) is one measure of physical adequacy which is then translated into potential profitability. The figure shows that at the end of 1977 the non-Communist world had approximately a thirty-three-year forward supply, almost the same as in the early 1960s. By 1980, with the addition of large Mexican and North Sea proven reserves, this worldwide R/P ratio will increase to a thirty-six- to thirty-seven-year forward supply. In fact, except for the mid to late 1950s, the expected 1980 ratio will be close to an all-time high. In the mid to late 1950s there was a worldwide oil glut, which is reflected in the more than forty years' forward supply during that period. As a result, world prices declined at that time, and exploration slowed until a more normal thirty-three- to thiry-five-year forward supply was achieved in the early to mid 1960s. The ratio has not really changed very much since then. The curve suggests neither shortage nor surplus, but a reasonable control by the unregulated market of worldwide oil inventories, albeit crude-oil inventories in known producing reservoirs.

With the advent of OPEC's monopoly pricing of world oil, however, the market price is kept artificially high. This will, in my opinion, induce surplus not shortage, as consumption becomes restricted and growing exploration indentifies increasing new supplies.

In the United States competition has forced an even tighter inventory control, so that proven reserves seldom exceeded twelve years of annual production. The much lower U.S. R/P ratio reflects a markedly different historical development of the oil industry in the United States from that which occurred overseas. Lower political risk, less volatile prices, and a much greater degree of competition either tended to reduce the need, or made it much more costly, to maintain as high an R/P ratio as was true overseas. The lower curve for the United States, however, measuring proven reserves to consumption (not production) has been declining. This is

Source: American Petroleum Institute.
[a] At Annual Consumption Rates.

Figure 1-2. Crude Oil, Years of Supply at Annual Production Rates

a reflection of a more difficult geological picture and a more costly operating environment. That is where U.S. price controls and a distorting regulatory policy come into play. As a result, one cannot be as optimistic about U.S. supply prospects as one can for the international outlook. The simple message for domestic policy is to deregulate, if not immediately at least gradually. The principal distortions of the competitive U.S. oil markets have come from overseas, from OPEC, and from relations between some international oil companies and some of the cartel governments. A mechanism is needed, therefore, to insulate the U.S. market as much as possible from these competitive distortions.

In sum, projected world oil shortages are analogous to a receding horizon; no matter how rapidly you move toward the horizon, it is still the same distance away. In my judgment, that analogy is more apt than one of a blind captain sailing his ship over the horizon where he falls off the world. Shades of Christopher Columbus!

Changing the Import Mechanism

Over the next few years the United States could become more rather than less dependent on foreign oil. But the particular problems in the United States notwithstanding, the very rise in world oil prices begun in 1974 is likely to lead to major oil surpluses around the world in years ahead. Both geology and economics support this view; it is largely political trends that suggest the scarcity theory. First, the world's proven reserves of crude oil were some 50 billion barrels higher in January 1979 then they were in January 1974, when the so-called energy crisis burst onto the scene. In other words, over the past five years new discoveries outpaced consumption by an average of 10 billion barrels per year, extending the world's future oil consumption horizon from about thirty-four years to thirty-six years. Second, new reserves from the North Sea and Mexico are likely to be identified rapidly over the next two to three years, so that the world's proven reserves will continue to increase faster than the world's consumption at least into the early 1980s. Third, to the extent that the geological concept of ultimately discoverable reserves is at all useful, the world is estimated to contain some additional 1.5 trillion barrels, or enough oil to last for another sixty-five years at projected future consumption rates. Fourth, with world economic activity likely to remain sluggish for some time ahead, there is little possibility of a major boom in petroleum demand. Finally, U.S. energy policy now appears committed to allowing substantially higher prices for newly discovered natural gas. The prospect of higher prices has encouraged significant new drilling which in turn could lead to a greater availability of natural gas, thereby arresting the trend toward substitution of oil for gas. While other energy sources, such as coal and nuclear power, remained mired in environmentalist controversy, drilling for new oil and gas in the United States and around the world is proceeding at a rapid pace.

The underlying premise of this book is that as a result of these forces there will be a continued easing of world oil markets. Not only will more abundant oil supplies offer the prospect of lower oil prices (in real terms), but they will create the environment in which the US. government could develop policies to dilute OPEC's price-setting powers. Within the context of this gradual shift of the world's oil markets toward excess supply, U.S. energy policy should seek to change the commercial mechanism by which oil is imported. Without this change, it is unlikely that oil consumers will benefit optimally from the improved market conditions.

To summarize the changes which I recommend, chapter 2 consists of my testimony before the U.S. Congress (Joint Economic Committee) in March of 1978. The major purpose of this book is to expand those recommendations, providing what I believe is a sound blueprint for national policy in this area.

Notes

1. Stewart L. Udall, *New York Times,* March 30, 1977, p. 27. © 1977 by the New York Times Company. Reprinted by permission. Udall was secretary of the interior from 1961 to 1969 and is now a Washington lawyer.

2. Analysis of Regional Incremental Costs of Oil and Gas: Derived from the NPC Oil and Gas Supply Model (Washington, D.C.; National Petroleum Council, 1972). I have updated the 1972 figures to account for both inflation and offsetting productivity gains.

Senate Testimony: Summary Policy Prescriptions

The principal objectives of government energy policy, within the limits of the immediate technical and political constraints, appear to me as follows: (1) Achieve the greatest possible independence from unreliable and monopoly-priced foreign oil sources. (2) Prevent energy shortages from causing increasing economic dislocations.

There are two separate sets of issues associated with the energy crisis. The first is an international problem, affecting U.S. foreign political and economic policies. These problems relate to the control of world oil supplies by the Organization of Petroleum Exporting Countries (OPEC), which represents a fundamental change in the world power structure. The second is a domestic economic problem, which is related to a changing set of social values among decision makers in the United States. Present energy policies have so confused these two sets of issues that neither objective is being met, and we are in fact further from them than we were in 1973. In particular, increasing constraints on domestic energy production have caused an even greater need to import oil from OPEC.

While this chapter stresses the international dimensions of the problem, I do not believe that actions on the international side alone will provide a panacea for our domestic energy problems. These domestic problems can be solved only by a combination of effective conservation policies and the timely development of alternate fuel sources, such as coal and nuclear power. Both of these fuel sources are mired today in environmentalist controversies and are not being developed rapidly enough to insure meeting the goals of the National Energy Plan. But there is also a more general energy problem related to the concept of energy conservation. Energy and economic growth are tied together; the so-called decoupling of energy and economic growth has some clear limits. A more efficient use of energy means sacrificing some growth in real personal income while capital investments for new energy conservation technology are implemented. Rising energy prices will continue to shift consumer spending to energy and other necessities whose production costs have risen due to energy costs. This means less growth in spending on other items. As a result, if general economic policy pushes too hard for a more rapid rate of real economic growth, severe infla-

Testimony of Dr. Arnold E. Safer before the Energy Subcommittee of the Joint Economic Committee on March 8, 1978.

tionary pressures will resume, and another economic recession may follow. Steady and slower growth is necessary until the economy can make the adjustments to these higher energy costs. Pushing too hard for a reduction in unemployment through higher government deficits will make the energy conservation job that much tougher. Between now and 1985 the economy will grow at a slower rate than during the past decade. The more rapidly it grows now, the greater the likelihood of a recession later. As a result, we may have to tolerate a higher level of unemployment for a few years until the growth of the labor force begins to slow in the early 1980s.

In terms of international issues, natural economic forces today are working toward a gradual reassertion of the market power of the oil-consuming nations. A slowing in the growth of world oil demand and the expected rapid increase in non-OPEC oil sources suggest that OPEC production peaked in 1977 and should gradually decline through the early 1980s. OPEC will be most vulnerable to consumer pressures during this period, since a number of the more heavily populated OPEC member nations will have an incentive to expand oil production at a time when world demand for total OPEC oil will be gradually declining. They can expand output only at the expense of the more sparsely populated OPEC countries. If Saudi Arabia reduces output to offset increased production by the more populous OPEC nations, it could be reduced to production levels which even it might find intolerably low. As another alternative, if Saudi Arabian production were held near current levels, other OPEC members would be forced to cut oil production below levels that would permit the planned implementation of economic development programs already in progress.

U.S. international oil policy should recognize the likelihood of this natural friction within OPEC. The period ahead offers the opportunity to limit the cartel's power over world oil pricing and to reach a healthier accommodation with the legitimate aspirations of its member governments.

I would like to turn now to the institutional mechanisms by which oil is imported into the United States and by which oil is priced on the international market. If the United States is likely to be importing substantial amounts of oil over the next decade, as I have projected, how can we stem the growing balance-of-payments drain on our domestic economy? Obviously, the first answer is to increase our exports of all goods and services, but a detailed examination of that issue is beyond the scope of this discussion. Second, we should conserve energy, and I believe that stronger measures are called for than the Congress is apparently willing to approve. A worldwide abundance of oil, as I projected, does not in any way lessen the need for a more energy-efficient economy. In addition to helping to slow the balance-of-payments drain, an effective conservation program would help dilute OPEC's monopoly price-setting capabilities. This leads me to the third and directly relevant factor; namely, we should seek a lower price for international oil or at least put into place new mechanisms that limit the capability of OPEC to further increase world oil prices. For example, in the international diplomatic arena it would be helpful to establish that some kind of market exchange system would be a better mechanism for determining the price of oil than an international treaty based on political perceptions of a fair price. The replacement cost of synthetic energy sources is not a realistic basis for oil pricing; nor is the indexing of oil prices to world inflation a useful departure point for international oil negotiations. Both pricing approaches make little economic sense in the long run and would simply add to the misallocation of the world's resources, both physical and financial. A market exchange system for oil, possibly regulated by representatives of both consuming and producing nations, would be a more useful approach. It is over the next few years, when the consuming nations may well be able to exercise significant market influence over the OPEC states, that this approach might be successfully applied.

To be specific, I would recommend a detailed examination and debate over the following complementary approaches for dealing with the monopoly power of OPEC. First, the present system of foreign tax credits under certain circumstances may help to link the interests of some international companies with those of some OPEC members. As a general proposition, the companies should be encouraged to bargain for crude oil at arm's length, thereby promoting competition among the OPEC states for world markets. The present system of foreign tax credits for certain crude-oil purchases may not be helpful in achieving that objective. Second, the U.S. government, together with other international financial agencies, should aid in the financing of oil exploration outside the U.S., primarily in the non-OPEC developing countries. The benefits of this policy should be apparent in terms of potentially adding to the world's supplies of oil and gas, in terms of relieving the balance-of-payments position of some of these countries, in terms of diluting some of OPEC's price-setting powers, and in terms of encouraging more competition in international oil markets. I believe that this additional financing should be complementary to the private sector, engaging perhaps in those ventures where the economic or political risks may be too great for private industry. Third, I support the ideas of Dr. M.A. Adelman of the Massachusetts Institute of Technology concerning the adoption of a bidding system for U.S. oil imports. Essentially, Adelman suggests that the U.S. government estimate our oil import needs and then use an auction technique to apportion that amount among would-be suppliers of imported oil. The competitive bidding for the right to sell this clearly defined quantity of oil would put each supplier under pressure to sell at a lower price in order to gain access to a larger share of the U.S. market. It seems to me that in the present surplus state of the oil market, this approach has an appreciable prospect for achieving success. Finally, the development of an organized exchange market for oil products would help to make the pricing process more competitive. There are some futures contracts for certain oil products now being developed by the commodities exchanges in New York. I believe that an open, visible pricing system for oil products would eliminate some of the need for excessive domestic regulation and thereby help both the Department of Energy and the oil companies. To the extent that a surplus appears in the market, the trading of the futures contracts will help to insure that oil prices react. If product prices decline because of slow volume, this will be felt by the refiners who will ultimately cut their production, which in turn will feed back to the crude suppliers. This process could then translate into lower crude-oil prices, as crude suppliers compete for market share.

None of these recommendations alone will likely be sufficient to dilute OPEC's hold on world oil prices. Taken together, however, they would certainly alter the expectations of oil market participants, both private companies and governments. Nevertheless, for the U.S. government to adopt these approaches, some of the concern over offending certain OPEC members would have to be reduced. Oil remains as much a commercial question as a political one. OPEC is a seller; the United States is a buyer. Our market interests, therefore, diverge. We can still be the best of political allies with the member governments of OPEC, but we can also bargain with them over the price of oil. I believe that the broad approach to international oil pricing problems should be to take the politics out of it as much as possible.

3   World Oil Outlook

In 1978 world oil consumption grew by only 1 million barrels per day, while non-OPEC oil supplies grew by close to 2 million barrels per day. Over the next five years world oil consumption will grow by only 4 million to 5 million barrels per day. At the same time the non-OPEC supplies could increase by as much as 7 million barrels per day. As a result, OPEC oil production will continue to decline, giving oil-consuming nations a major opportunity to dilute some of OPEC's monopoly price-setting powers.

In April of 1977 President Carter declared that the energy crisis facing America was the "moral equivalent of war." The basis of his statement and his program of energy conservation was a prediction of a worldwide shortage of energy, in particular a shortage of crude oil. The president declared that by 1985 the world would face a situation where demand for oil exceeded available supplies, and prices would rise to such alarming proportions that the world's economies would be brought to a grinding halt. Subsequent events are pointing in the opposite direction, namely, toward an abundance of world oil supplies in the mid 1980s.

Economists and geologists can debate the issue of scarcity versus abundance without reaching any firm conclusions. Neither science is sufficiently advanced to be able to tell what the oil supply situation is likely to be ten or fifteen years from now. We can, however, make some sense out of the shorter-term, four- to five-year outlook. The reason for this difference is really very simple. Current exploration for oil or gas may or may not be successful; no one really knows today what potential hydrocarbons exist in the vast unexplored regions of the world. If new supplies are not found, then the world will face a growing scarcity in the late 1980s or 1990s. If, on the other hand, current exploration is successful, there could be oil surpluses around the world ten to twenty years from now. In the shorter run, however, we can make reasonable judgments about the extent to which currently known reservoirs will be developed. For the next five years both economics and geology point toward abundance, not scarcity.

What is the outlook for the next five years? To what extent will the world continue to depend on OPEC for its oil supplies and therefore on OPEC-determined oil prices? The answer depends on predictions of demand growth and the availability of non-OPEC supplies.

World Oil Consumption

The worldwide demand for energy has slowed dramatically since 1973. From 1960 to 1973 oil consumption in the non-Communist world grew at an annual rate of around 7.5 percent, the result of a worldwide economic boom fueled in part by cheap energy supplies. From 1973 to 1977 oil consumption grew at only 1 percent per year, the result of a worldwide economic slump caused in part by energy costs five to six times their previous levels. Over this four-year period oil consumption in the United States grew at around 1.2 percent per year, declining in 1974 and 1975 but rising as the economy expanded in 1976 and 1977. In Western Europe oil consumption actually declined over this four-year period, while Japanese oil consumption stayed essentially flat. Estimated 1978 world oil consumption is only 2 percent above 1977, down sharply from the 5 percent growth experienced in 1977 and the 7 percent growth of 1976. In other words, as economic activity picked up after the world recession of 1974–1975, oil consumption followed suit. In 1978, however, growth in oil consumption did not keep pace with continued economic expansion.

Figure 3–1 shows a projection of world oil consumption to 1983. While the economic outlook for 1979 and 1980 is for sluggish growth in the United States, the economies of Western Europe and Japan can be expected to exceed the rates achieved over the 1973–1977 period. Based on projected economic growth rates in the 3 percent per year range for the 1977–1980 period, growth in world oil consumption is likely to exceed the rate achieved over the 1973–1977 period, rising by an expected 2 percent per year over this period. In the longer run, however, over the 1980–1983 period, the effects of conservation will begin to take hold. Despite an anticipated acceleration of economic growth, oil consumption is likely to grow at an even slower pace in the 1980–1983 period. In the United States, for example, growth of motor gasoline consumption will slow to under 2 percent in the 1980–1981 period and will be flat in the 1982–1983 period. The congressional mandate to Detroit to improve the mileage efficiency of the average new car sold to 27.5 miles per gallon by 1985 has now been augmented by the "gas-guzzler" tax, thereby accelerating the process toward reduced gasoline consumption. In the industrial and commercial sectors, greater fuel efficiencies can be expected, not only in the United States but also in Western Europe and Japan. As a result, the amount of oil used per unit of real output will be declining in the 1980–1983 period.

Figure 3–2 shows the relative growth in real gross national product (GNP) and in oil consumption over the historical periods 1970–1973 and 1973–1977 and over the future periods 1977–1980 and 1980–1983. World economic growth is expected to show continued expansion during the 1977–1980 period and to accelerate even more markedly during the 1980–1983

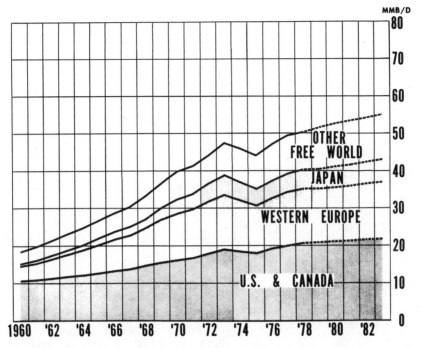

Source: Historical data from *International Petroleum Encyclopedia;* projections by the author.

Figure 3-1. World Oil Consumption

period. Nevertheless, because of greater fuel efficiencies, growth in oil consumption per unit growth in real GNP is likely to fall over this period. While world GNP is expected to grow by 3.0 percent per year over the 1977–1980 period and by 3.5 percent per year over the 1980–1983 period, oil consumption is projected to increase by only 2 percent per year and 1.5 percent per year over the same time periods.

Non-OPEC Oil Supplies

In 1973 non-OPEC supplies were 18.6 million barrels per day (MMB/D) (including net Sino-Soviet exports to the non-Communist world), while world oil consumption was 48.8 MMB/D. (Tables 3A-2 and 3A-3 explain the difference between petroleum product consumption and refinery demand for hydrocarbon raw materials; see tabular appendix to this chapter.) By 1978 non-OPEC supplies had increased to an estimated 22.1 MMB/D, while world consumption had grown to an estimated 50.3

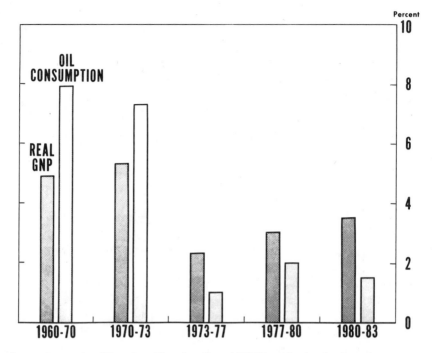

Source: *International Petroleum Encyclopedia* and OECD; projections by the author.
Figure 3–2. World Oil Consumption and Economic Growth

MMB/D. In other words, over the past five years oil consumption has grown by little more than 1.5 MMB/D, while non–OPEC supplies have increased by more than 3.5 MMB/D. That trend will continue in 1979. An increase of almost 1.5 MMB/D in non–OPEC supplies can be expected in 1979, with the major gains from the North Sea and Mexico partially offset by continuing declines in the lower forty–eight states.

Figure 3–3 shows a projection of non–OPEC oil supplies to 1983. Several key assumptions underlie these estimates. (See Tabular Appendix to chapter 3.) First, continuing declines can be expected in oil production in the lower forty–eight states through 1980. It appears that despite an almost 20 percent per year increase in U.S. drilling rates since 1973, U.S. production in the lower forty–eight states has continued to decline at an annual rate of some 200 to 300 thousand barrels per day.

It is impossible to sort out precisely how much of this decline is due to technical problems, regulatory impediments, or market conditions. The decline in the lower forty–eight states comes from the "old oil" category, now called "lower tier" because of the low price that is imposed by federal price controls. At the same time, "stripper oil," from wells producing less than 10 barrels per day has been increasing at least partially because this category of oil production is essentially decontrolled and commands a price

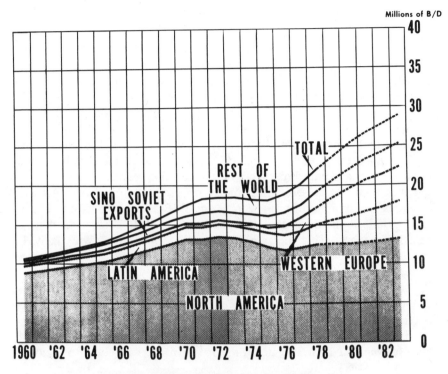

Source: Historical data from *Petroleum Institute;* projections by the author.

Figure 3-3. Non-OPEC Oil Production

more than 2.5 times as high as the lower tier oil. In addition, because of U.S. government regulations, the perverse incentive remains to hold back the marginal domestic barrel and increase the marginal foreign barrel. Finally, the West Coast surplus is forcing a shut-in of substantial amounts of oil production from California oil wells owned by independent producers. Because Alaskan crude oil came into the California market before imports were substantially reduced, local California oil was displaced from the market. The profit incentive to some California refiners remains with foreign oil. For these reasons, lower forty-eight state production can be expected to continue to decline through 1980. If price controls and entitlements are eliminated, however, there is reason to believe that lower forty-eight state production could at least hold steady after 1980. By 1981 most U.S. oil will command world market prices, simply because much of the lower-priced old oil is rapidly disappearing. In addition, present legislation provides a reasonable prospect of achieving total oil price decontrol by 1981. To the extent that the price incentive for new natural gas is now in place, there should be some additional natural-gas liquids produced as new gas supplies come to market in the early 1980s. Stepped-up advanced recovery methods and some of the first shale oil production will also add marginally to lower forty-eight state supplies by 1981.

There is no geological impediment to increasing Alaskan or Canadian production. Current transportation difficulties surrounding increased oil production from the Alaskan North Slope can be resolved by 1980 or 1981. This could involve a temporary exchange agreement with Japan, especially since Mexican oil, likely to be shipped to Japan by that time, could be easily traded for North Slope oil. Part of this transportation problem may also be resolved by the Long Beach, California, pipeline project, recently approved by the voters in an open referendum. In Canada the discoveries at West Pembina and Elmworth could add several billion barrels of proven reserves, while Athabascan tar sands production is expected to increase by several hundred thousand barrels per day over the next five years.

As a result of these considerations, oil production in North America can be expected to stabilize at around 12.5 MMB/D between 1978 and 1980, and by 1983 it should increase by another 0.7 MMB/D to more than 13 MMB/D a year. This increase in Canadian production will likely be exported to the United States, as Ottowa's autarkic energy policies become increasingly vulnerable to balance-of-payments pressures.

In Western Europe North Sea oil production continues to increase, albeit at a slower pace than had been expected. The advent of major production from the Ninian field should help to increase British North Sea production substantially in 1979. By 1980 the combined output of the British and Norwegian North Sea should reach 3 MMB/D and climb to almost 4 MMB/D by 1983.

In Latin America Mexico is rapidly emerging as an oil superpower. Proven reserves have increased from 2 billion barrels in 1974 to an estimated 30 billion barrels in late 1978; based on these proven reserves alone, oil production could reach 5 to 6 MMB/D by 1985. By then, however, it is likely that the proven reserves will be much larger than is currently known, since the possible oil reserves have been estimated at over 100 billion barrels. A conservative view of Mexican oil production suggests that 2.2 MMB/D is likely by 1980 and at least 3 MMB/D by 1983.[1] In 1977 other non–OPEC Latin American nations produced over 1.2 MMB/D. These include the Caribbean (300,000 barrels per day), Brazil (200,000), Argentina (400,000), Columbia (150,000), and Peru (200,000). Current trends suggest that these production rates will increase to 1.6 MMB/D by 1980 and 2 MMB/D by 1983.

Other non–OPEC areas in the non–Communist world produced over 2.5 MMB/D in 1977. These include non–OPEC African countries (700,000 barrels per day), non–OPEC Mideastern nations (600,000), India and the Far East (800,000), and Australia–New Zealand (400,000). By 1983 these areas should add another 1 MMB/D to non–OPEC supplies.

Probably the single most controversial area of new non–OPEC supplies is the magnitude of Sino–Soviet exports. Contrary to popular belief, Russian exports to the West are increasing, not decreasing. This is in sharp contrast to the well-publicized Central Intelligence Agency (CIA) report cited by President Carter at the time of his energy proposals to the American public in April of 1977. The CIA suggested in that study that the Soviet Union would turn from a net exporter of 1.5 MMB/D in 1975 to a net importer of 2 to 3 MMB/D by 1985. Since the CIA study was issued, a number of critical reviews have found serious fault with the CIA's assumptions. In particular, there is no firm reason to believe that Soviet production will decline significantly. But even if it were to fall off, the Soviets' need for hard Western currencies suggests that they would continue to export oil and substitute coal and nuclear fuel for domestic energy needs.

In 1977 Russian oil exports of both crude and products, net of imports, were higher than had been reported previously.[2] They include over a half a million barrels a day of petroleum products exported by Russian or Eastern European refineries to Western nations but are based largely on Russian crude oil or natural-gas liquids. In 1978 total net Sino-Soviet exports to the West were estimated to reach 2 MMB/D. By 1980 expanding Chinese and Soviet production could increase these exports to 2.5 MMB/D; by 1983 they could reach 3 MMB/D. These projections of rising exports are based on a recent report by a group of Swedish consultants, which suggested that the CIA report, predicting declines in Soviet production, was a complete misinterpretation of Soviet conditions.[3] Although efficiency and infrastructure need to be improved, vast areas are still unexplored. More important for the next five years, the Soviets are now concentrating on boosting production from known fields that had been systematically underproduced by 30 percent in Western Siberia and had not been worked at all in European Russia. Chinese exports, which went largely to Japan, reached 200,000 barrels per day in 1977. By 1983 these exports will easily reach 500,000 barrels per day. Add to this outlook the recent reports of new oil finds in China, and a picture of Sino-Soviet exports to the West emerges that is totally different from the one portrayed by the CIA in the summer of 1977.

In toto, figure 3-3 projects an increase of almost 7 MMB/D in new non-OPEC supplies between 1978 and 1983. Compare this projection to the actual increase of only 3.6 MMB/D in new non-OPEC supplies between 1973 and 1978. That is a projected doubling over the next five years. Given the accelerated pace of worldwide oil drilling and the admittedly long lead times required to bring production on-stream, it is not unreasonable to project that more new oil supplies, rather than less, will be available, at least between 1978 and 1983.

Estimating oil production beyond 1983 is only guessing at what might be discovered in still unexplored regions. Many significant potential pools of new oil and natural gas are known to geologists. These include offshore Argentina, Vietnam, the U.S. East Coast, Alaska, and northern Canada.

(Significantly for the U.S. picture, the East Coast exploratory drilling started in early 1978, but it will be several years before commercially producible hydrocarbons can be definitively established.) Policymakers cannot count on new reserves coming from these areas, but neither can they discount them. Yet longer–term (more than five–year) projections are made, and they normally forecast a decline in reserves. A forecast of declining non–OPEC world oil supplies by 1985 is only a projection that existing reserves will gradually deplete over time; it is also an assumption that no significant reserve additions will be made during that time. Private oil companies sometimes project declining reserves more than five years out, but when they do, they use the forecasts as the basis for budgeting funds for exploration. They confidently assume that the exploration will lead to new discoveries that will make the original forecasts obsolete. When governments make such projections of declining reserves, they tend to draw doomsday conclusions from them. The latest scare is only one of many during this century. In 1914, 1926, and 1949 the U.S. government became seriously concerned over impending oil shortages; each time, though, their fears were premature. At some future time, of course, oil will be a relatively scarcer commodity than it is today, but that day will not come as soon as many think.

OPEC Oil Supplies

OPEC oil production reached its peak in 1973 at close to 31 MMB/D. OPEC maintained roughly this rate in 1974, but production declined substantially in 1975 with world recession. OPEC oil production rebounded to 30.5 MMB/D in 1976 and exceeded 31 MMB/D in 1977.

Figure 3–4 shows that in 1973 and 1974 OPEC production reached two-thirds of world consumption. In 1975 world oil consumption declined as a result of recession. OPEC production declined even more, and the OPEC proportion of total world demand fell to less than 60 percent. With economic recovery in 1976 and 1977, world demand and OPEC production have expanded at about the same rate, and the OPEC proportion has remained at slightly above 60 percent.

In 1977 OPEC production came to 31.2 MMB/D. Since world consumption was only 49.5 MMB/D and non–OPEC supplies were 20.1 MMB/D, an excessive inventory buildup took place at the end of 1977, amounting to about 1.8 MMB/D. These stocks were rapidly worked off in the first half of 1978, and OPEC production over the January–June period fell to some 28.5 MMB/D. In the second half of 1978 a similar inventory buildup took place. Over and above the seasonal inventory swing, oil purchases from OPEC accelerated in the latter half of 1978 as a result of indus-

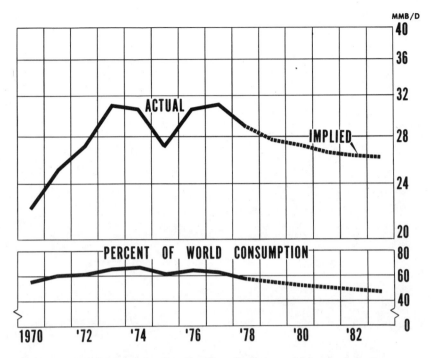

Source: Historical data from *American Petroleum Institute;* projections by the author.
Figure 3-4. OPEC Oil Production

try anticipation of another price increase. Strikes by Iranian oil workers, the Saudi decision not to expand production of light crude oils, and the confusion caused by the greater than expected consumption of unleaded gasolines all compounded the sense of market scarcities in the last months of 1978. OPEC production averaged an estimated 31.3 MMB/D for the second half of 1978, so that average OPEC production for the full year came to about 29.9 MMB/D. My estimate of average 1978 consumption at 50.5 MMB/D and non-OPEC production of 22.1 MMB/D would therefore imply a year-end inventory buildup of around 1.5 MMB/D, almost as much as had occurred a year earlier. Another surplus could occur late in 1979 or in 1980, if Iran comes back to full production at the same time as a surge of new North Sea oil comes to market.

The forecast of future OPEC production is derived from the difference between projected world consumption and projected non-OPEC production. Table 3-1 shows a substantial decline projected for OPEC production in the 1980-1983 period, when OPEC could be supplying half of world consumption, down sharply from the two-thirds they actually supplied in 1973

Table 3–1
Actual versus Implied OPEC Production
(in millions of barrels per day)

	1973	1974	1975	1976	1977	Estimated 1978	Projected 1979	Projected 1980	Projected 1983
World consumption	47.3	45.9	44.1	47.2	49.5	50.5	51.5	52.5	55.8
Less: Non-OPEC supplies	18.5	18.2	18.1	18.9	20.1	22.1	23.8	25.3	28.9
Implied OPEC Production	28.8	27.7	26.0	28.3	29.4	28.4	27.7	27.2	26.1
Actual OPEC Production	31.0	30.7	27.1	30.6	31.2	29.9			
Share of consumption (%)									
Implied production	61	60	59	60	59	56	54	52	47
Actual production	66	67	61	63	63	59			

and 1974. This table shows an estimate of implied OPEC production to 1983. The difference between implied and actual results from annual inventory swings, but it is the implied figures that suggest the longer-run pressures on OPEC production rates. Since the implied figures are the differences between projected world consumption and projected non-OPEC production, they represent a scenario of potential challenge to the dominance of the oil cartel. In 1973 and 1974 OPEC accounted for almost two-thirds of world consumption; by 1983 this figure could fall below 50 percent, hardly the market conditions conducive to monopoly pricing.

The figures for implied OPEC production are not a prediction of what will occur. Aside from inventory swings, OPEC production could be altered by several other factors. Pricing and politics will affect how much each OPEC member in fact produces, especially those sparsely populated countries in the Arabian Peninsula and North Africa. These five countries (Libya, Kuwait, Qatar, the United Arab Emirates, and Saudi Arabia) represent 50 percent of OPEC production. They have literally all the spare capacity to increase production if they choose—or to cut production to insure the OPEC pricing structure.

Table 3-2 shows the distribution of actual OPEC production in 1977. Note that total OPEC production was split about evenly between the large and small population groups. As total requirements for OPEC oil begin to decline over the next few years, however, OPEC will be faced with a fundamental challenge to its internal cohesion. Some member countries will have to cut back oil production in the face of rising import costs, thereby jeopardizing development programs already in progress. The way for any one OPEC country to maintain its oil exports in the face of declining demand, however, would be to cut prices, and the incentive to do so will grow as excess capacity builds over the next few years. To prevent this OPEC would either have to set up a centralized allocation system or agree to lower prices for all member countries in an attempt to stimulate overall demand for OPEC oil. The adoption of either alternative will further erode OPEC unity and will mean increased bargaining power for consuming countries.

Figure 3-5 and table 3-2 show that the average production rate projected for OPEC oil during the period 1980-1983 is 26.5 MMB/D. Case A assumes that Saudi Arabia and the other small-population OPEC countries absorb the major portion of the decline in the need for OPEC oil, diminishing their proportion of total OPEC production to around 32 percent. This would leave 68 percent to the large-population OPEC countries. The problem with this scenario is, however, that it requires an average Saudi Arabian production rate of only 4 MMB/D, which is too low for even the wealthy Saudi princes. This permits Iran and Iraq to maintain, or even to increase, their market shares and thus to continue to pursue their economic and political objectives, at the possible expense of Saudi Arabia.

For Saudi Arabia an average production rate over four years of 4

MMB/D would entail a major loss of cash flow and force significant changes in their plans for economic development. This loss of revenues would also mean a loss of political influence, worldwide and especially among the Arab states. The Saudi's, therefore, are unlikely to cut back to below a 7 MMB/D production rate, as shown in case B. This would still maintain their economic and political objectives, albeit at a somewhat strained rate, as world inflation continues to erode their purchasing power. The estimate of a minimum Saudi production rate of 7 MMB/D is further supported by evidence from the Saudi–Aramco negotiations, which call for the Aramco partners (Exxon, Mobil, Texaco, and Standard Oil of California) to buy at least 7 MMB/D from the proposed fully Saudi–owned Aramco. In other words, the Saudi's have insisted that these companies maintain purchases in this range, or the financial compensation to the companies will be reduced.

Case B puts the pressure on Iran, which could be forced down to a 3.5 MMB/D rate over an extended period. This production rate is probably too low for whatever new government might emerge in Iran. It is unlikely that any new Iranian government would permit oil production to be reduced sufficiently to accommodate even this minimum desired level of Saudi production. How these two major oil exporters resolve this impending dilemma will determine the future of OPEC and the direction of world crude prices.

One answer would be to reduce OPEC prices and thereby limit the growth of non–OPEC supplies over the next few years. This reduction could take place in real terms by freezing the nominal OPEC price or at least by not permitting the OPEC price to rise as fast as worldwide inflation. This strategy will maintain the growth of purchasing power in the industrial economies, permit renewed growth in the developing countries, and be a continued source of stability for the world financial system. Yet it is not likely to occur as long as the OPEC cartel continues to exercise its monopoly control over world oil prices, a situation which is tolerated, if not encouraged, by the governments of the oil–consuming nations.

The two cases outlined here are clearly untenable polar extremes, designed to suggest the inherent friction likely to arise within OPEC. U.S. foreign policy should recognize the possibility that this potential instability within OPEC could lead to political repercussions in the Mideast. Present foreign policy perceptions concerning the Mideast are clouded by the official forecast of increasing world energy scarcity and thus tighter OPEC control over world oil supplies in the mid 1980s.

A Historical Perspective

The abundance of crude oil in world markets over the past year and a half has been called a temporary situation that will disappear in the mid 1980s.

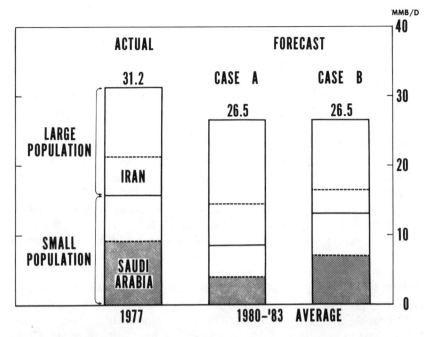

Source: Historical data from *American Petroleum Institute;* projections by the author.
Figure 3–5. Distribution of OPEC Oil Production

Table 3–2
Distribution of OPEC Production
(in millions of barrels per day)

	1973	1977	Forecasted 1980–1983 Average	
			Case A	Case B
Saudi Arabia	7.6	9.2	4.0	7.0
Iran	5.9	5.7	6.0	3.5
Other small–population group	5.2	4.4	4.5	6.0
Other OPEC	12.3	11.9	12.0	10.0
Total	31.0	31.2	26.5	26.5

To the extent that one can forecast with tolerable accuracy over a four- to five-year period, oil markets are likely to remain in relative abundance, not shortage. What happens beyond that time depends largely on current exploration and cannot be quantified with sufficient precision to become a guide for policy.

As a result of the recent political upheavals in Iran, which have sharply curtailed Iranian oil production, the OPEC ministers have mandated a substantial increase in oil prices for 1979. Nevertheless, economic logic points to an abundance of world oil for many years to come, precisely because of the existence of the OPEC cartel. As long as OPEC keeps prices above their competitive market levels, consumers will use less than they otherwise would and new supplies will become ever more profitable under the protection of the cartel's price umbrella.

Between 1963 and 1973 the world's appetite for oil soared by 26 MMB/D, double the rate of consumption of the prior decade. Almost 80 percent of this increase in demand was supplied by OPEC, giving the cartel the power which it exercised so forcefully in 1973 and 1974. Over the past five years the world's oil consumption has increased by only 1.5 MMB/D, while non-OPEC supplies have increased by 3.5 MMB/D. This has reduced the market power of the cartel, and it is a trend that will continue. Over the next five years I expect at most a 5 MMB/D increase in world oil consumption, provided the world's economies remain reasonably healthy. If there is a world recession, oil demand would grow at an even lower rate, although the economic and political costs to the West could be severe. At the same time, I expect an increase of almost 7 MMB/D in non-OPEC supplies (table 3-3). These could be further augmented by new discoveries in China, Africa, Latin America, or even the United States. Thus the pressure on OPEC's market power will continue, thereby offering the consumer of oil increasing leverage to bargain down the price of oil in the marketplace. The opportunity is here; we should take advantage of it now.

Table 3-3
World Oil Supply and Demand Changes, Past and Future
(in millions of barrels per day)

	Demand	Non-OPEC Supply	OPEC Supply
1963–1968	10.2	3.5	6.8
1968–1973	16.0	2.9	13.1
1973–1978	1.6	3.6	−2.0
1978–1983 (projected	4.5	6.8	−2.3

Notes

1. That Mexico will in fact seek to expand its oil exports significantly is demonstrated by an interesting quote from Diaz Serrano, director general of Petroleos Mexicanos: "Either we produce the oil now, without delay and without childish fears, using it already as far as our strength and intelligence allow it, to be really self-sufficient and sovereign, or pretty soon we will deplore not having been up to the historic time we are living in." (Report of the Director General of Petroleos Mexicanos, March 18, 1978, Mexico City, on the commemoration of the fortieth anniversary of the nationalization of the petroleum industry.)

2. *Business Eastern Europe,* October 6, 1978, p. 314.

3. "Soviet Preparations for Major Boost of Oil Exports"; *Petro-studies,* Malmo, Sweden 1978.

Appendix 3A
Tabular Appendix

Table 3A-1
Oil Consumption and Economic Growth, Average Annual Growth Rates
(in percents)

	1960–1970		1970–1973		1973–1977		1977–1980		1980–1983	
	Real GNP	*Oil Consumption*	*Real GNP*	*Oil Consumption*	*Real GNP*	*Oil Consumption*	*Real GNP*	*Oil Consumption*	*Real GNP*	*Oil Consumption*
United States	4.0	4.0	4.7	5.7	1.9	1.2	2.0	1.5	3.0	1.0
Western Europe	4.9	12.5	4.6	5.4	1.9	−0.7	3.0	1.0	3.5	1.5
Japan	11.1	19.2	8.7	12.1	3.1	0.0	4.5	4.0	5.5	3.0
Total[a]	4.9	7.9	5.3	7.3	2.3	1.1	3.0	2.0	3.5	1.5

Source: Historical data from U.S. Department of Commerce and *International Petroleum Encyclopedia*; projections by author.
[a]OECD, plus estimate for developing countries.

31

Table 3A-2
World Oil Demand, Historical and Projected
(in millions of barrels per day)

	United States	Canada	Western Europe	Japan	Other	Total
1955	8.5	0.5	2.0	0.2	.9	13.1
1960	9.8	0.8	3.8	0.7	3.4	18.5
1965	11.5	1.1	7.5	1.7	4.9	26.7
1970	14.7	1.5	12.7	4.0	7.0	39.9
1973	17.3	1.6	14.6	5.0	8.8	47.3[a]
1974	16.7	1.6	13.9	4.9	8.8	45.9
1975	16.3	1.6	13.2	4.6	8.4	44.1
1976	17.1	1.7	13.4	4.8	10.2	47.2
1977	18.4	1.7	14.0	5.0	10.4	49.5
1978 estimated	18.7	1.7	14.2	5.2	10.7	50.5
forecast:						
1979	19.0	1.8	14.3	5.4	11.0	51.5
1980	19.3	1.8	14.4	5.6	11.4	52.5
1981	19.5	1.8	14.6	5.7	11.7	53.3
1982	19.7	1.9	14.8	5.9	11.8	54.1
1983	20.0	1.9	15.0	6.1	12.0	55.0

Source: Historical data from American Petroleum Institute and *International Petroleum Encyclopedia;* projection by author.

Note: Figures excluding Communist nations.

[a] Demand here is defined as raw material requirements at refineries and other processing plants; demand differs from petroleum product consumption by the change in inventories. In 1973 as a result of the oil embargo and the decline in production, there was a reduction of petroleum product inventories by an estimated 1.5 MMB/D. Consumption was therefore an estimated 48.8 MMB/D, rather than the official figure given above at 47.3 MMB/D. Due to the Iranian crisis of late 1978, a similar process seems to have occured, with a markedly lower than usual year-end inventory buildup.

Table 3A-3
Raw Material Production, Refinery Demand, Petroleum Consumption, and Inventories: Non-Communist World
(in millions of barrels per day)

Year	Refinery Raw Material Demand	=	Petroleum Product Consumption	+	Petroleum Product Inventory Changes
1973	47.3		48.8	−	1.5
1974	45.9		43.7	+	2.2
1975	44.1		44.4	−	0.3
1976	47.2		46.3	+	0.9
1977	49.5		48.4	+	1.1
1978 estimated	50.5		50.3	−	0.2

Table 3A-3 (cont'd)

	Refinery Raw Material Demand	=	Raw Material Production	−	Raw Material Inventory Changes
1973	47.3		49.5		2.2
1974	45.9		48.9		3.0
1975	44.1		45.2		1.1
1976	47.2		49.5		2.3
1977	49.5		51.3		1.8
1978 estimated	50.5		52.0		1.5

Source: Author's estimate of inventory changes.

Table 3A-4
Non-OPEC Oil Production, Historical and Projected
(in millions of barrels per day)

	North America	Latin America	Western Europe	Rest of World	Net Sino-Soviet Exports	Total
1960	8.8	0.9	0.3	0.1	0.4	10.5
1965	10.3	1.0	0.4	0.2	0.9	12.8
1970	13.2	1.5	0.4	1.4	1.0	17.5
1971	13.2	1.5	0.5	1.7	1.4	18.3
1972	13.5	1.6	0.5	1.7	1.2	18.5
1973	13.4	1.5	0.5	1.9	1.2	18.5
1974	12.9	1.6	0.6	1.8	1.3	18.2
1975	12.2	1.8	0.6	2.0	1.5	18.1
1976	11.8	1.9	1.1	2.3	1.8	18.9
1977	12.1	2.1	1.7	2.6	1.7	20.2
1978 estimated	12.5	2.6	2.2	2.8	2.0	22.1
forecast:						
1979	12.5	3.1	2.9	3.0	2.3	23.8
1980	12.5	3.5	3.6	3.2	2.5	25.3
1981	12.7	4.0	4.0	3.3	2.7	26.7
1982	12.9	4.3	4.2	3.5	2.9	27.8
1983	13.2	4.7	4.4	3.6	3.0	28.9

Source: Historical data from American Petroleum Institute and *International Petroleum Encyclopedia;* projections by author.
Note: Figures include crude oil, condensate, natural-gas liquids, and refinery processing gains.

Table 3A-5
North American Oil Production, Historical and Projected
(in millions of barrels per day)

	U.S. Lower 48 States	Alaska	Canada	Total
1960	8.3	—	0.5	8.8
1965	9.5	—	0.8	10.3
1970	11.8	—	1.4	13.2
1971	11.7	—	1.5	13.2
1972	11.8	—	1.7	13.5
1973	11.5	—	1.9	13.4
1974	11.1	—	1.8	12.9
1975	10.6	—	1.6	12.2
1976	10.4	—	1.4	11.8
1977	10.3	0.2	1.6	12.1
1978 estimated	9.9	1.1	1.5	12.5
forecast:				
1979	9.6	1.3	1.6	12.5
1980	9.3	1.5	1.7	12.5
1981	9.0	1.7	2.0	12.7
1982	9.0	1.8	2.1	12.9
1983	9.0	2.0	2.2	13.2

Source: Historical data from American Petroleum Institute; projections by author.
Note: Figures include crude, condensate, natural-gas liquids, and refinery processing gains.

Table 3A-6
Western European Oil Production, Historical and Projected
(in millions of barrels per day)

	Great Britain	Norway	Other[a]	Total
1960	—	—	0.3	0.3
1965	—	—	0.4	0.4
1970	—	—	0.4	0.4
1971	—	—	0.5	0.5
1972	—	—	0.5	0.5
1973	—	—	0.5	0.5
1974	—	—	0.6	0.6
1975	—	—	0.6	0.6
1976	0.2	0.3	0.6	1.1
1977	0.8	0.3	0.6	1.7
1978 estimated	1.1	0.4	0.7	2.2
forecast:				
1979	1.6	0.6	0.7	2.9
1980	2.0	0.9	0.7	3.6
1981	2.2	1.0	0.8	4.0
1982	2.3	1.1	0.8	4.2
1983	2.4	1.2	0.8	4.4

Source: Historical data from *International Petroleum Encyclopedia;* projections by author.
[a] Figures include crude oil, natural-gas liquids, and estmated refinery processing gains.

Table 3A–7
Latin American Oil Production, Historical and Projected
(in millions of barrels per day)

	Mexico	Brazil	Argentina	Other	Total
1960	0.3	0.1	0.2	—	0.9
1965	0.3	0.1	0.3	0.1	1.0
1970	0.4	0.2	0.4	0.5	1.5
1971	0.4	0.2	0.4	0.5	1.5
1972	0.4	0.2	0.4	0.6	1.6
1973	0.5	0.2	0.4	0.4	1.5
1974	0.5	0.2	0.4	0.5	1.6
1975	0.7	0.2	0.4	0.5	1.8
1976	0.8	0.2	0.4	0.5	2.1
1978 estimated	1.5	0.3	0.4	0.4	2.6
forecast:					
1979	1.9	0.4	0.4	0.4	3.1
1980	2.2	0.4	0.5	0.4	3.5
1981	2.5	0.5	0.5	0.5	4.0
1982	2.8	0.5	0.5	0.5	4.3
1983	3.0	0.6	0.6	0.5	4.7

Source: Historical data from *International Petroleum Encyclopedia;* projections by author.
Note: Figures exclude Venezuela and Ecuador, which are members of OPEC.

Table 3A–8
Rest of World Production [Non–Communist, Non–OPEC], Historical and Projected
(in millions of barrels per day)

	Africa[a]	Mideast[b]	Asia and Oceania	Total
1960	—	—	0.1	0.1
1965	0.1	—	0.2	0.2
1970	0.4	0.5	0.5	1.4
1971	0.5	0.5	0.7	1.7
1972	0.4	0.5	0.8	1.7
1973	0.4	0.5	1.0	1.9
1974	0.4	0.5	0.9	1.8
1975	0.5	0.6	0.9	2.0
1976	0.6	0.7	1.0	2.3
1977	0.7	0.7	1.2	2.6
1978 estimated	0.8	0.7	1.3	2.8
forecast:				
1979	0.9	0.7	1.4	3.0
1980	1.0	0.7	1.5	3.2
1983	1.3	0.7	1.6	3.6

Source: Historical data from *International Petroleum Encyclopedia;* projections by author.
[a] Includes Egypt and Sinai.
[b] Includes Syria, Turkey, and Oman.

Table 3A-9
Communist Area Production, Consumption, and Exports; Historical and Projected
(in millions of barrels per day)

	Production			Total	Consumption	Net Exports
	USSR	China	Other			
1950	0.8	—	0.1	0.9	0.9	—
1960	3.0	0.1	0.2	3.3	2.9	0.4
1965	4.9	0.2	0.3	5.4	4.5	0.9
1968	6.2	0.3	0.2	6.7	5.7	1.0
1969	6.6	0.4	0.3	7.3	6.3	1.0
1970	7.1	0.5	0.3	7.9	6.9	1.0
1971	7.5	0.7	0.4	8.6	7.2	1.4
1972	8.0	0.8	0.4	9.2	8.0	1.2
1973	8.6	1.0	0.4	10.0	8.8	1.2
1974	9.2	1.2	0.4	10.8	9.5	1.3
1975	9.8	1.6	0.4	11.8	10.3	1.5
1976	10.4	1.7	0.4	12.5	10.7	1.8
1977	10.9	1.8	0.4	13.1	11.4	1.7
1978 estimated	11.5	2.0	0.4	13.9	11.9	2.0
forecast:						
1979	11.8	2.2	0.4	14.4	12.1	2.3
1980	12.0	2.9	0.4	15.3	12.8	2.5
1981	12.5	3.1	0.4	16.0	13.3	2.7
1982	13.0	3.3	0.4	16.7	13.8	2.9
1983	13.5	3.6	0.4	17.5	14.5	3.0

Source: Historical data from *International Petroleum Encyclopedia;* projections by author.
Note: Exports are derived from the difference between production and consumption.

Table 3A-10
OPEC Production and Share of World Market, Historical and Projected

	Production (MMB/D)	Proportion of World Consumption (%)
1970	22.1	56.4
1971	25.1	60.8
1972	27.1	61.5
1973	31.0	65.5
1974	30.7	66.9
1975	27.1	59.4
1976	30.6	63.2
1977	31.2	63.2
1978 estimated	29.9	59.2

Table 3A-10 (cont'd)

forecast:[a]

1979	27.7	52.8
1980	27.2	51.8
1981	26.6	50.0
1982	26.3	48.6
1983	26.1	47.4

Source: Historical data from *International Petroleum Encyclopedia;* projections by author.

Note: Figures exclude Communist countries.

[a] Forecasted OPEC production is the difference between world consumption and non-OPEC production, referred to as "implied" in the text. The difference between implied and actual would be accounted for by inventory changes.

Table 3A-11
Distribution of OPEC Projection, Actual and Projected

	Actual 1977		Forecasted 1980-1983 Average			
			Case A		Case B	
	(MMB/D)	(%)	(MMB/D)	(%)	(MMB/D)	(%)
Large population group						
Algeria	1.0	3.2	1.1	4.2	1.1	4.2
Equador	0.2	0.6	0.2	0.8	0.2	0.8
Gabon	0.2	0.6	0.2	0.8	0.2	0.8
Indonesia	1.7	5.5	2.0	7.5	2.0	7.5
Iran	5.7	18.3	6.0	22.6	3.5	13.2
Iraq	2.4	7.7	3.5	13.2	2.5	9.4
Nigeria	2.1	6.7	2.5	9.4	2.0	7.5
Venezuela	2.2	7.1	2.5	9.4	2.0	7.5
Total	15.5	49.7	18.0	67.9	13.5	50.9
Small population group						
Libya	2.1	6.7	1.5	5.7	1.9	7.2
Kuwait	2.0	6.4	1.5	5.7	1.9	7.2
UAE and Qatar	2.4	7.7	1.5	5.7	2.2	8.3
Saudi Arabia	9.2	29.5	4.0	15.1	7.0	26.4
Total	15.7	50.3	8.5	32.2	13.0	49.1
Total OPEC	31.2	100	26.5	100	26.5	100

Source: Historical data from *International Petroleum Encyclopedia;* projections by author

Adjustment in the World Economy

Although the magnitude of surplus OPEC petrodollars will not in itself destroy the international financial system, the burden of recycling these funds to deficit nations has put severe strains on the world's economies. Ever-rising world oil prices are a major cause of unemployment and inflation in Western nations. As long as the terms of trade continuously shift in favor of the OPEC nations, the economic prosperity of the oil-consuming countries will be undermined.

The value of the U.S. dollar in foreign exchange markets has become a major casualty of the oil crisis. Since the dollar is the world standard of value, its decline has caused an erosion of confidence among our major trading partners and political allies.

The world has not really adapted to the increased price of international oil imposed by the cartel of oil-producing nations. The mounting international debt of many developing countries and of some industrialized nations is one important symptom of the disruptive nature of high oil prices. As long as large OPEC surpluses continue, there will be an ever-increasing burden of deficits in the oil-importing nations that must be financed through the international monetary system. Chronic international payments deficits can set off a vicious devaluation-inflation cycle, which in turn brings about high unemployment or increased protectionism—key symptoms of the failure of the economic adjustment process. Most economic historians feel that the failure of the international economic and financial system was a principal element in the Great Depression of the 1930s. Measures taken in the 1930s to defend against these deficits emphasized exchange controls and protectionist trade policies which contributed to a sharp contraction in world trade, an end to economic prosperity, and the ultimate rise of destructive economic nationalism.

The world has learned much about economic cooperation since the 1930s, and economic history shows that many of the aspirations of individual OPEC nations cannot be achieved except at considerable expense to the rest of the world. The strategy of achieving economic development by imposing high oil prices on the rest of the world contains certain risks to OPEC as well as to the oil-consuming nations, both developed and developing. The world recession of 1974–1975 was in large part the result of the oil price shock; the slow recovery of the world's economies may be another. But it is precisely this slow economic recovery, with its limitations on increasing social goals, that may well cause the gradual erosion of the strength of the cartel itself. It is important for both Western policymakers and the governments of OPEC to understand this process. The economic process depends critically on three related forces: first, the state of the oil market and the resulting pressures on oil prices; second, the magnitude of the OPEC petrodollar surplus and the distribution of the corresponding deficit among oil-consuming nations, both industrial and developing; and third, the manageability of the system by which these petrodollars are recycled in the context of national economic aspirations and the interdependence of the world economy.

World Oil Markets

As has been emphasized in chapter 3, it is likely that natural economic forces are working today toward a gradual reassertion of the market power of the oil-consuming nations. A slowing in the growth of world oil demand and the expected rapid increase in non-OPEC oil sources suggest that OPEC production peaked in 1977 and should gradually decline over the next several years. OPEC will be most vulnerable to consumer pressures during this period, since a number of the more heavily populated OPEC member nations will have an incentive to expand oil production at a time when world demand for total OPEC oil will be gradually declining. They can only expand output at the expense of the more sparsely populated OPEC countries. If Saudi Arabia alone reduces output to offset increased production by the populous OPEC nations, its production could be reduced to levels that even it might find intolerably low. As another alternative, if Saudi Arabian production were held near its average level in 1978, other OPEC members would be forced to cut oil production below levels that would permit the planned implementation of economic development programs already in progress.

Over the next five years OPEC's minimum production level required to sustain its member countries' respective development objectives will continually rise with world inflation (figure 4-1). This estimate is based on assessment of each country's oil-producing capacity in comparison with its foreign exchange needs to import Western goods and services. If the projected rate of 26 to 27 million barrels per day (MMB/D) for OPEC production over the 1980-1983 period is realistic, then the world would need from OPEC less than this minimum production level. This difference between the amount of OPEC oil that the world *must have* and the amount of oil that OPEC *must sell* will have declined from almost 15 percent in 1973-1974 to

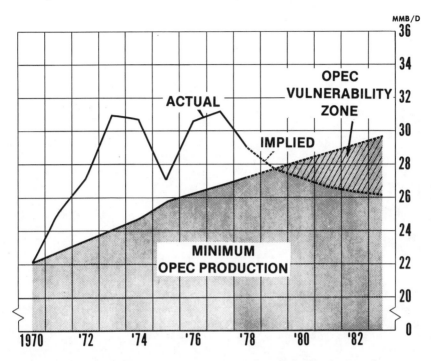

Source: Historical data from *American Petroleum Institute;* projections by the author.
Figure 4-1. OPEC Oil Production

zero by 1979; in 1980 and beyond, it could be negative. The sudden rise in oil prices caused by the turmoil in Iran will accelerate world inflation, causing even higher OPEC foreign exchange needs. At the same time, demand for OPEC's oil will decline further, putting even greater pressure on the cartel's cohesion.

Magnitude of Petrodollars

This forecast has important implications not only for oil prices but also for the health of the world's economies, primarily reflected by the size and distribution of the OPEC petrodollar surplus or its opposite side, the petrodollar deficit. Prior to 1974 the OPEC financial surplus came to about $15 billion, largely concentrated in Saudi Arabia and Kuwait. By the end of 1977 this figure had risen to about $175 billion, with Saudi Arabia alone accounting for roughly 60 percent of this total. By the early 1980s this petrodollar surplus will likely level off at just over $200 billion (figure 4-2).

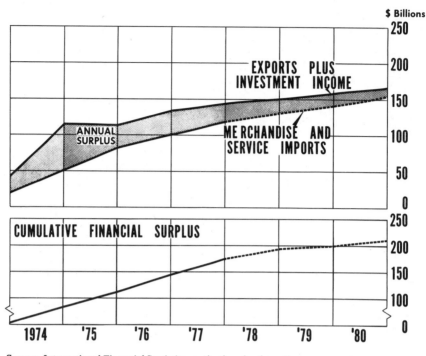

Source: *International Financial Statistics*, projections by the author.
Figure 4-2. OPEC's Financial Surplus

In effect, virtually the entire surplus will be concentrated in the small population OPEC members, principally the Arab states of the Persian Gulf. At
the same time, some of the large–population OPEC members could go into
substantial current account deficit over the next few years.

The petrodollar issue has now assumed a dimension different from that
initially perceived. Several years ago the fears of the financial community
were focused both on the magnitude of the surplus petrodollars likely to
build up and on the mechanism by which they would be recycled. The first
problem has now receded because it has been recognized that the cumulative
OPEC surplus will not build into the completely unmanageable trillion-
dollar range by 1980 but will likely be more in the neighborhood of $200 bil-
lion. Although some observers have suggested that this smaller sum can be
managed without excessive strain on the private financial system, even that
proposition is now open to question. The stronger industrialized countries
have generally been able to maintain a reasonable balance of trade among
themselves. Thus the annual OPEC surplus has become, on balance, a burden for the less competitive industrial countries, for the developing nations,

Table 4-1
OPEC Current Account and Cumulative Financial Surplus

	1977	1980	1982
	(actual)	(projected)	
Oil production (billion bbls)	11.1	10.2	9.5
Domestic use (billion bbls)	0.7	1.0	1.2
Oil exports (billion bbls)	10.4	9.2	8.3
Oil prices ($/bbl) [a]	12.04	14.00	15.50
Value of oil exports ($billion)	125.2	128.8	128.7
Other exports ($billion)	15.0	22.0	25.0
Investment income ($billion)	9.0	18.0	23.0
Total OPEC receipts ($billion) [b]	149	169	177
Merchandize imports ($billion)	83	110	125
Service imports ($billion) [c]	37	45	50
Current account balance ($billion)	29	14	2
Cumulative financial surplus ($billion) [d]	175	210	215

[a] Government take, average OPEC. International crude-oil prices are assumed to rise 5 percent to 1982.

[b] Rounded to nearest billion.

[c] Includes transfers from OPEC to other nations.

[d] Year-end figures; 1973, $15 billion; 1976, $145 billion.

and increasingly for the Communist bloc. The continuing ability of these countries to finance their trade deficits has now become the chief concern of the financial community. In other words, the problems now center largely around the world distribution of the balance-of-payments deficits and the methods by which these are being financed.

Table 4-1 translates my forecast of OPEC oil production into OPEC oil revenues. I have assumed an increase of 5 percent per year in oil prices after 1977. As a result of the expected decline in OPEC volume, therefore, OPEC oil revenues are projected to grow only marginally through the remainder of the decade. With a continued rise in merchandise and service imports, OPEC is likely to experience a decrease in its annual current account surplus through 1982. The cumulative financial surplus is therefore expected to peak at just over $200 billion in the 1980-1982 period.

By the end of 1978 the cumulative outstanding debt of the non-oil developing countries is estimated at close to $300 billion, with approximately $120 billion owed to commercial banks, both in the United States and overseas. For the past five years this group of countries has required over $30 billion annually in external financing, with the majority of that need stemming from current deficits rather than from the financing of long-term development programs. This annual flow of resources to the developing nations totals about 1 percent of the non–Communist world's gross national product (GNP). Although this figure may not seem excessive, there has been a concentration of this flow in the form of increased loans from private Western banks to the developing countries. While I do not believe that this represents an inordinate level of risk at present, further expansion of private–sector lending to the developing countries could pose problems for the future.

Thus petrodollar recycling is in fact occurring. The question is how vulnerable is the process to unpredictable events such as political upheavals, international currency problems, and protectionist trade policies. In effect, OPEC is forcing the Western nations, both governments and private institutions, to co–sign the check on the flow of their surplus to the deficit countries.

Economic Effects of Petrodollars

The OPEC financial surplus is one measure of the degree to which the growth in real consumer purchasing power has been reduced by the necessity to pay more for oil, leaving less for the purchase of other goods and services. To the extent that this surplus is likely to decline over the next several years, the drag on world purchasing power will diminish and the potential for greater real growth will be enhanced. Nevertheless, this rapid buildup of financial claims by certain key OPEC states against the oil–consuming nations will represent a cumulative deficit of more than $200 billion over the period 1973–1980. After 1982 this petrodollar overhang (OPEC surplus equaling the oil–consuming nation's deficits) could recede, provided that oil prices stabilize. The Persian Gulf countries' oil exports will stabilize while their industrial imports will continue to grow, as their economic development accelerates into the takeoff stage. Until that time, however, the world will continue to be faced with the intractable problems of simultaneous inflation and recession, caused at least in part by the rapid rise in oil prices and the inability of certain OPEC states to spend these vast sums.

To what extent is the current international economic malaise related to the energy problem? Since the rise in oil prices and the buildup of the OPEC petrodollar surplus, the world's economies have been suffering from "stagflation," a combination of sluggish real economic performance and sharply higher rates of inflation. In Europe and Japan historical growth rates have been more than halved; in the United States inflation is more than double its long–term average.

The conventional tools of countercyclical economic policy do not easily lend themselves to combating these dual diseases of high inflation and stagnating real economic performance. Because of the energy-related adjustment problem, consumers must continually pay a greater proportion of their budget for energy and postpone or reduce the purchase of other goods and services. This relatively inelastic consumer response to energy use means that nonenergy businesses do not experience sufficient demand growth to expand capacity. The result is that such businesses attempt to maintain profit margins through higher prices rather than higher volume. Therefore, to maintain growth in purchasing power, governments must increase their budget deficits, feeding the fires of inflation. As the inflation accelerates, real consumer purchasing power is diminished and recessionary forces reappear. Thus the adjustment process has become one of more pronounced oscillation between inflation and recession. Maintenance of steady, noninflationary economic growth sufficiently rapid to absorb the growing labor force of the industrial world has become a much more difficult task, owing to the pressures of high energy prices.

While environmental delays and regulatory rigidities have exacerbated the adjustment process, they are transient rather than fundamental barriers. The deeper problem lies in OPEC control of world oil prices. As long as OPEC can obtain increase in oil prices at rates higher than those of world inflation, the terms of trade will continuously shift in their favor, aggravating the stagflation in the consuming countries. To the extent that OPEC can increase oil prices only at rates lower than world inflation, the terms of trade will shift gradually in favor of the oil-consuming nations, releasing more real consumer purchasing power for non-oil goods and services. This is the fundamental adjustment process that I believe is now taking place.

But it is a painful process and one fraught with political risks. Democratic governments cannot easily withstand the forces of stagflation, because their political processes are inherently more cumbersome than those of totalitarian states. Thus government policies have become more unstable, and democratic societies have become more difficult to govern. This is true both in the United States and overseas. Eurocommunism still represents a threat to European democracies, while in Japan the fear of rising unemployment has become a serious barrier to the elimination of import restrictions.

The effects of these forces on each domestic economy have meant greater competition for world markets. Higher costs of doing business, coupled with sluggish growth in the volume of world trade, have caused growing protectionist sentiment both in the United States and abroad. Japanese policies designed to stimulate exports but restrain domestic consumption have led to massive Japanese trade surpluses, causing resentment and potential protectionist reaction in the United States and Western Europe. From 1955 to 1973 world trade grew in real terms at an average annual rate of 8 percent; since 1973 this figure has barely exceeded 4 percent per year. As a result, attempts to expand economic growth through international trade have become difficult options for major trading nations. This problem has become especially acute for non-oil producing developing countries with only limited export flexibility. These countries are forced to pay more for oil, while at the same time they experience a decline in the effective demand for their agricultural and other commodity exports because the countries to which they export are also paying more for oil.

Another important casualty of the energy crisis is the value of the U.S. dollar in international financial markets. While some of this decline might have occurred without the rapid rise in oil prices, it is certainly true that the present cost of U.S. oil imports has severely exacerbated this dollar depreciation. This has caused further disruption in world trade, as businessmen and government officials seek stability from widely fluctuating international currency values. Floating exchange rates may have been a valid response to the breakdown of dollar dominance under the Bretton Woods system, but the advent of OPEC oil pricing has caused unacceptable volatility in this system. As the recycling of surplus OPEC petrodollars to deficit oil-consuming nations becomes the principal theme of international financial transactions, world governments have found it difficult to manage the floating rate system to prevent chronic payments imbalances, which after all was the original raison d'être for the conversion from fixed to floating rates.

Is the System Manageable?

The present approach to international economic policy runs along two complementary lines. First, there has been a continuation of recycling, but the burden has increasingly shifted to governments and international financial institutions and away from reluctant private sources. Governmental lending has the advantage of providing the governmental body with greater leverage in imposing constraints on the domestic economic policies of the borrower—essentially an insistence that the borrower keep down the growth of domestic demand, which in many less developed countries can mean severe limitations on their aspirations for economic development. This approach has often been accompanied by sharp declines in the value of the borrowing nation's currency, as investors become concerned about the country's economic prospects and as the borrowing country's government seeks to promote exports and restrain imports. The result is often an even more depressed economy, with consumers unable to spend and business unwilling to invest. The resulting improvement in the balance-of-payments position may ultimately bring about renewed growth, provided that the world economy as a whole generates sufficient growth to restimulate demand for the borrowing country's exports.

Enter the second element of international economic policy now being pursued by the Carter administration. The proposition is that the surplus industrial countries (Japan and West Germany) should further stimulate their economies with the objective of creating balance-of-payments deficits. Easier fiscal and monetary policies in the surplus countries will lead to an increased level of imports, and a part of these increased imports will likely be exports from the deficit countries, either directly or indirectly. For example, as the United States stimulates its domestic economy, it buys more commodities directly from the developing countries as well as more consumer goods from Japan. Japan, at the same time, increases its imports of raw materials from the developing nations, thereby generating a strong second-order effect on the exports of the deficit countries.

This two-pronged approach of restraint in the deficit countries and stimulus in the surplus countries may help to gradually restore a measure of equilibrium to the international payments mechanism. The petrodollar recycling is basically a credit flow, a series of loans to carry the deficit countries through their period of adjustment. That, however, could be the fly in the ointment. The growing deficits of the weaker countries may be none too temporary as long as OPEC continues to run these very large balance-of-payments surpluses stemming from the high and still rising price of oil. There is reason to believe that increased stimulus in the stronger countries will not lead to an improvement in the weaker countries.

The effect could be an increased world deficit vis-a-vis OPEC, as stronger economic growth worldwide in both the surplus and the deficit countries generates a sharply increased demand for oil. When the United States, for example, stimulated its economy in 1977 and 1978, this move led not only to an increase in U.S. imports from the deficit countries but also to an increase in the demand for Japanese goods. At the same time, both Japan and the United States increased their oil imports. As the developing countries increase their raw material exports to the United States and Japan, they may end up with even higher deficits as their economies begin to require more oil and more industrial goods at even higher prices. In other words, the proposal assumes a fairly constant OPEC surplus to be redistributed among oil-consuming countries. Unless worldwide energy conservation and U.S. domestic energy development receive greater attention, the increased tempo of economic activity and world inflation could generate an even larger OPEC surplus and leave all oil-consuming countries with an even larger petrodollar deficit.

Another problem with the proposed course of international economic policy involves the value of the dollar in foreign exchange markets. With an increased U.S. balance-of-trade deficit, the international value of the dollar has weakened substantially, despite offsetting capital flows. The cost of U.S. non-oil imports has risen, as it now takes more dollars to purchase foreign goods from other countries. The result has been increased inflationary pressures in the domestic U.S. economy. As the yen and the mark strengthen relative to the dollar, the U.S. economy has, at least in the short run, been importing inflation from abroad. We may be accomplishing the goal of reducing the deficits of the developing countries, at least temporarily, but we are at the same time also giving a new inflationary underpinning to our own economy and further increasing the surpluses of Germany and Japan.

Whether or not the foreign economic policy of the United States follows this internationalist course, the underlying problem, namely, the high price of oil and the control of that price by an international cartel, will not be eliminated. A system of financial transfers from the surplus industrial countries to the deficit countries, both developed and developing, may not lead to a correction of the economic imbalances unless this underlying cause is removed. Thus energy policy should become an integral part of economic policy, both internationally and domestically. The international component of that policy must be to seek a reduction in the growth of world oil prices through dilution of OPEC's monopoly control over the marketplace. Without this element of policy, stimulating the world's economies in the interest of promoting higher levels of employment runs the serious risk of renewed world inflation and ultimately another, perhaps even deeper, world recession. Economic growth may have to be slower than in the past, with more attention paid to the capital needs of the world economy, so that energy-conserving and new energy-producing technologies will be in place to gradually reduce the world's dependence on OPEC oil.

5

U.S. Policy Options: Economic and Political Realities

Although the world as a whole will have an increasing abundance of oil, the United States will still be faced with a domestic scarcity of petroleum. If we must import it, we should learn to buy it better.

U.S. government regulations have so distorted business incentives in the domestic oil industry that imports are encouraged and domestic production is discouraged. Energy policy should focus on the international oil markets where the monopoly control of OPEC can be diluted through stimulation of competition among its members.

The U.S. government should simultaneously remove all price controls from U.S. oil markets and subsidize the purchase of foreign oil. Technically this is a more efficient system of holding down U.S. energy costs and of changing the commercial mechanism by which oil is imported into the United States.

Table 5-1 shows that U.S. oil imports have risen from 6.3 million barrels per day (MMB/D) in 1973 to an estimated 8.0 MMB/D in 1978. By 1983 U.S. oil imports will be about 9.5 MMB/D, even with the slowing of

Table 5-1
U.S. Demand, Supply, and Imports
(in millions of barrels per day)

	1973 (actual)	1978 (estimated)	1983 (forecasted)
Consumption	17.3	18.7	20.0
Strategic reserve	—	+ 0.3	+ 0.5
Demand	17.3	19.0	20.5
Production	11.0	11.0	11.0
Imports	6.3	8.0	9.5
OPEC	4.4	7.0	6.5
Non–OPEC	1.9	1.0	3.0
Canada	1.3	0.3	0.5
Mexico	—	0.2	1.5
Other	0.6	0.5	1.0

demand growth and the availability of more gas supplies. Over the decade 1973-1983 U.S. oil imports will grow about as much as the increase in demand, with Alaskan production approximately offsetting the decline in the lower forty-eight states.

However, between 1973 and 1978 U.S. imports from OPEC increased by almost 3 MMB/D, while non-OPEC imports declined, largely owing to declining Canadian production. By 1983 increased production in Canada, Mexico, and other areas (North Sea, Sino-Soviet) could mean increased U.S. imports from non-OPEC sources. As table 5-1 suggests, between 1978 and 1983 the United States could reduce its dependence on OPEC from 85 percent to 70 percent of its total oil imports. This diversification of import sources should be a major policy goal, since it would not only add to the competitive pressures on OPEC but would also reduce the risks to the United States of unforseen supply interruptions.

The commercial terms of these oil imports after 1980 could be quite different from present terms. First, if OPEC is supplying less than half of the world's oil demand by the early 1980s, versus more than 60 percent today, then the cartel may have a more difficult time in maintaining its internal cohesion and could become more susceptible to arm's-length bargaining over crude-oil prices. Second, if non-OPEC foreign sources are providing 30 percent of world demand by the early 1980s, versus less than 20 percent today, then a greater number of oil import sources will be available than at the present time.

To take advantage of these changes, the United States should give serious consideration to altering the commercial mechanism by which oil is imported. Over the next few years as OPEC's alternatives become more limited, other pricing options might become more acceptable to them, and U.S. international oil policy should focus on setting the stage for a new approach to oil pricing. It should also continue a dialogue with the oil-exporting nations that might lead to OPEC's recognition of the mutual gains that a neutral market pricing system could provide.

U.S. action on the international aspects of oil pricing, however, will become effective only when there is equally effective action on the pricing of domestic oil. Yet a major source of confusion in the U.S. government's oil policy stems from differing, and often conflicting international versus domestic objectives. On the international side OPEC monopoly pricing is the central issue, and the government has partially sheltered the U.S. consumer from high prices by imposing price regulations on domestic oil. But on the domestic side the single most important aspect of the energy problem is how to increase domestic oil supplies. The price regulations imposed domestically have so distorted the U.S. oil situation that domestic supplies are not increasing as rapidly as they might. Nor are they likely to as long as the strongly market-oriented oil industry expects continued price regulation.

As a result, I propose the substitution of more involvement by the U.S. government in international oil for less government regulation of the domestic oil business. The proposal attempts to isolate the domestic oil business from the international distortions caused by OPEC. In particular, an enlarged government role is suggested for setting the volumes and prices at which oil is imported. In return, I recommend that all domestic oil be deregulated. This can be achieved at no direct increase in cost to the U.S. consumer. This approach does not call for confrontation with OPEC governments but would rest partially on their cooperation. This is a more easily administered plan with less bureaucratic control of U.S. crude-oil prices and the prospects of producing more U.S. oil.

In particular, this proposal would accomplish the following objectives:

Limit OPEC's influence on U.S. energy prices.

Lead to some alteration of existing oil company-OPEC relationships.

Remove distortions from the U.S. domestic oil market caused by excessive regulations, and so promote a more rapid increase in domestic oil prices.

Enable the U.S. government to better control the cost of oil to the U.S. consumer (the mechanism of this control would be neutral with respect to the use of higher prices for achieving conservation goals).

Potentially ease the growing international debt burden of the developing countries.

A Regulatory Quagmire

The Energy Conservation and Policy Act of 1975 (ECPA) was a compromise between the Republican administrations's desire to remove price controls from domestic crude oil and the Democratic Congress's desire to hold down domestic crude-oil prices in the interest of the U.S. consumer. The resulting law forced down U.S. crude-oil prices to $7.66 per barrel and permitted escalation of these average prices by a maximum of 10 percent per year. Due to administrative delays and regulatory confusion, the original plan to remove price controls from U.S. oil by 1979 is now projected at 1981. To implement the ECPA the Federal Energy Administration (now absorbed into the Department of Energy [DOE]) constructed a multitier system of domestic crude-oil prices, where "old" oil (from wells producing before January 1, 1973) can sell at prices no greater than $5.25 per barrel, while various tiers of newer oil and "stripper" oil (oil from wells producing less then 10 barrels per day) are allowed to sell at significantly higher prices, but still generally below the world market. The administration of this program has become so confusing and costly that it is itself a strong impediment to increased U.S. crude-oil production.

An even more serious indictment of this regulatory mess is the imposed system of entitlements, where the DOE attempts to equalize the cost of crude oil to all purchasing refineries. An oil company with access to a larger-than-average amount of cheaper domestic oil, to refine that oil must pay a premium to refiners having access to a smaller-than-average amount of domestic oil. An exchange of funds occurs when refiners with large amounts of cheaper domestic oil buy entitlements from firms with smaller amounts. Only by purchasing these entitlements can they refine more than a DOE-determined average amount of domestic crude oil. This system has markedly increased U.S. oil imports. To avoid being penalized for processing domestic crude-oil, companies with both overseas and U.S. production have a strong incentive to import more foreign oil and produce less domestic oil than they would under market-determined prices. Refiners with little access to domestic crude-oil use the premiums paid to them for the entitlements to increase their imports. Since their increased imports enlarge the ratio of foreign to domestic oil that determines the amount of their entitlements, it further increases the subsidy that they receive from their competitors.

The entitlements system, coupled with crude-oil price controls and historical allocations, is locking the entire crude-oil market into a fixed pattern of purchases and sales, guaranteeing substantial penalties to those who produce more domestic oil. As a result, imports are encouraged and domestic production is discouraged.

The heavy hand of regulation on what was a reasonably open market has severely distorted expectations of profit and loss. New investment in the oil business has always been based on the anticipation of both high risks and high rates of profitability. At the exploration and production end the geological risks are high, while rising capital costs have substantially increased the business risks. In the refining business the elaborate control system has seriously impeded investment in new capacity. Unpredictable regulations have added a further degree of uncertainty. Market incentives have been severely diluted and competition blunted because the drive for more efficient business has been stifled by fear that regulations will penalize those who take a chance to get ahead of their competition. The state of expectations in a market-oriented economy is not easily measurable but is very real to those whose capital is at risk.

Shielding the U.S. Consumer

On the other hand a strong case for continued price controls on crude oil has been made on both equity and economic grounds. A recent study at the

U.S. Treasury suggests that because of OPEC price increases the real output of the U.S. economy is 7 percent to 8 percent less than it would have been without those increases. The study goes on:

> If we continue along our present trends of energy consumption and production, and OPEC continues to raise prices by 5 to 10 percent each year, then by 1985 the real output of our economy will be another 4 to 5 percent below the level it would have achieved if OPEC prices would have remained constant.[1]

It is also true that on equity grounds, higher energy prices have severely hurt lower income groups. Even with controls on U.S. crude-oil prices, the direct cost of energy to the consumer has risen from about 3 percent of disposable income in 1973 to 7 percent in 1977. At the same time, the secondary effects on prices of all goods and services has probably had at least as great an impact as the direct effect. For those families with incomes under the $15,000 national median, rising energy costs have become a heavy burden. As a result, there is a natural political impetus to share these burdens more equitably within the total population.

Emotional Pressures

An additional force for continued price regulation stems from the perception by many in Washington that the oil industry was at least partially responsible for OPEC's success in raising international oil prices. This perception is a very real threat to the oil industry, no matter what the truth of the situation. As a result, oil price controls have a punitive aspect, due to the widespread belief that the oil companies made excessive profits on the high energy prices imposed by OPEC.

International Considerations

During the past several years there has been increasing awareness that the world economy has not really adjusted to the high price of crude oil imposed by OPEC. High oil prices are at least partly responsible for the intractable slow growth and high inflation now besetting much of the industrial world. The international financial problems of recycling surplus petrodollars are clearly related to the inordinately high price of oil. These issues have now surfaced in a variety of ways. Deficit industrial countries are leaning toward protectionist trade policies; the developing countries have increased their international indebtedness to private Western banks to historically high levels; and the U.S. government is now trying to promote more rapid growth rates among the surplus industrial countries, paying insufficient heed to the oil–related inflation–recession consequences of that policy.

Consequently, there is an increasing perception that the real price of oil will have to fall. This can probably occur only as a result of a gradual decline in the use of oil. Conservation will help to some extent, but a stagnating world economy is more likely until new energy supplies can be made available in the quantities required to supplant OPEC oil at prices that reflect economic costs. Faced with these harsh realities, a strong case can and should be made for attempting to dilute OPEC's pricing powers and not continuing to rely on traditional OPEC–oil company relationships in imported oil transactions.

Proposed Changes in U.S. Oil Policies

I recommend the following set of specific steps that the U.S. government should take toward solving some of these problems.

Subsidize the cost of oil imports to reduce the price of foreign oil to the U.S. consumer. The U.S. government should deal directly with the governments of OPEC in negotiating these payments. In return for these payments the governments of OPEC would reduce their selling price to the international oil companies, who in turn would pass on the full amount of the subsidy to the U.S. consumer. To the extent that some OPEC members might keep the subsidy and demand the full price from the oil companies, the U.S. government could pay the oil companies directly, so that no change in the payments arrangement to OPEC need occur.

Remove all price controls from the U.S. oil market. The average price of domestic oil would rise to the ceiling imposed by the import subsidy, so that foreign and domestic oil would sell at the same price in the United States, with no increase in the overall direct cost to the U.S. consumer. The price of international oil should not be affected by the manner in which the oil payments to OPEC are made, whether totally by the oil companies or partially by the U.S. government.

Impose an extra–profits tax on domestic oil producers, with a full reinvestment credit for increased exploration and production. If there is no increase in domestic drilling, the U.S. Treasury would get back the cost of the import subsidy. If the oil companies increase their U.S. drilling, the Treasury would get back less revenue but would have the prospect of more domestic oil.

Impose a variable oil–import quota to prevent anyone from taking unfair advantage of the import subsidy and to enhance the U.S. government role in choosing the amounts and sources of foreign oil. As market conditions change, the size of the quota can be adjusted. As U.S. oil production grows over the next decade, the quota can be reduced, decreasing the overseas subsidy payments made by the U.S. Treasury.

Rationalizing the Crude-Oil Market

In 1978 the U.S. consumed 6.8 billion barrels of oil of which 4.0 billion barrels, (59 percent) was domestically produced. The U.S. consumer paid an average $9.90 per barrel for the domestic oil and $14.00 for the imported oil (at the crude-oil equivalent cost of the product imports). This was a weighted average price of $11.59 per barrel. Foreign oil cost $39.2 billion and domestic oil $39.6 billion.

Under my proposal the consumer would have paid the same $11.59 per barrel average price but in a different way. Suppose the U.S. Treasury had paid foreign oil-exporting governments $2.41 per barrel directly, either in cash or in long-term Treasury notes. In return for this payment the OPEC governments would have agreed to reduce their price to the purchasing oil companies by an equivalent amount. The price of imported oil in the United States would then have fallen to $11.59 per barrel. If, at the same time, there had been no controls on the price of domestic oil, the U.S. crude-oil market would have risen to this average of $11.59 per barrel, from the controlled price of $9.90. As a result, domestic producers would have increased their profits by $1.69 per barrel, an apparent windfall caused by the higher foreign price and the removal of controls. If this $1.69 per barrel were subject to an extra-profits tax, unless it were entirely reinvested in domestic drilling, then these profits could be used to the advantage of the U.S. public by stimulating an increase in the search for more U.S. oil. If these profits were not reinvested, they would have been taxed away, helping the U.S. Treasury pay the foreign oil-exporting governments.

The burden of the plan would have fallen on the U.S. Treasury, which would have controlled both the import price differential and the extra-profits tax. If reinvestment of these extra domestically earned profits had been high, the Treasury would have received back less revenues but would have had the prospect of more domestic oil. If reinvestment had been low, the Treasury would have received most of the funds to pay for the import subsidy.

Furthermore, if oil-exporting governments had been willing to take a U.S. Treasury note instead of cash, the U.S. taxpayer would not have had to pay the full OPEC price immediately. Such a transaction would represent a future OPEC claim on U.S. goods and services and would be similar to OPEC investment in the United States.

What would this plan have achieved? First, it would have lifted all direct price controls from the U.S. crude-oil market, eliminating the multi-tier price structure and the entitlements program. It would have restored a competitive open market for crude oil in the United States, rewarding the risk taker and penalizing those committed to the windfall profits resulting from regulations. All crude oil in the United States would have been uniformly priced, subject to normal quality and location differentials. The control of U.S. prices would have been achieved through the international import price differential, which is where U.S. government action should be taken, since the objective of price control is to shield the U.S. consumer from OPEC-dictated prices. U.S. response to OPEC is primarily an international problem and should be dealt with through international economic policy. The present approach confuses this issue with the domestic energy problem and is thereby exacerbating the domestic situation by imposing the heavy weight of government regulations on the domestic oil industry.

This plan does not deal directly with the problem of how to cope with OPEC monopoly pricing. The approach is technical in nature and simply substitutes a more rational regulatory method for the present one. Nevertheless, the proposal does indirectly affect U.S.-OPEC relations and could be used to alter some of the existing oil company-OPEC arrangements. For example, the imposition of a variable import quota would be necessary to prevent an increase in imports of the subsidized foreign oil. Since the U.S. Treasury would be making the import price differential payments to the OPEC governments directly, the government would be increasingly involved in oil company-OPEC negotiations. Thus the U.S. Treasury would be able to encourage imports from one OPEC country rather than another by varying the magnitude of the import price differential.

Judicious use of this import price differential would resemble some of M.A. Adelman's recommendations. Dr. Adelman of the Massachusetts Institute of Technology has suggested that the U.S. government estimate the nation's oil import needs and use an auction technique to apportion that amount among would-be suppliers of imported oil (an import quota system). The competitive bidding for the right to sell this clearly defined quantity of oil would put each supplier under pressure to sell at lower prices to gain access to a larger share of the U.S. market. My proposal that the U.S. government set an import price differential, payable to OPEC governments, would reverse the Adelman approach as long as the international crude-oil market had substantial excess demand. If and when excess supplies appeared, my proposal could revert to the Adelman format.

This plan is not designed to answer the question of how high U.S. oil prices should be to induce the necessary conservation. The proposed mechanism for control of crude-oil prices is neutral with respect to the use of higher prices for achieving conservation goals. Increases in the price of crude oil from its current level are unlikely to have substantial or immediate impact on product prices and therefore on consumption. For example, even if all U.S. crude-oil prices were to rise from their present $10 per barrel average to $14 per barrel, this would cause an increase of only about five cents per gallon in gasoline prices—hardly enough to change most people's driving habits.

What this plan does offer is a more easily administered and less bureaucratic means of controlling U.S. crude-oil prices and the prospect of more U.S. oil by stimulating more domestic drilling at no extra direct cost to the consumer. It effectively insulates the U.S. crude-oil market from the rest of the world and permits normal domestic market expectations to function appropriately. Figure 5-1 is a pictorial illustration of this proposal.

Future Oil Policy

Table 5-2 contains a projection of U.S. oil demand and supply between 1979 and 1983. U.S. imports over the five-year period are projected at 3.2 billion barrels per year. Domestic production is expected to rise gradually over the period, averaging 3.9 billion barrels per year. Foreign oil prices are forecast to increase by about 5 percent per year over the period, and to

U.S. consumes 7 billion barrels per year at an average of $11/bbl. Assume a 50-50 split between domestic oil and imports, so that the $77 billion is divided into $46 billion foreign ($13/bbl.) and $31 billion domestic ($9/bbl.)

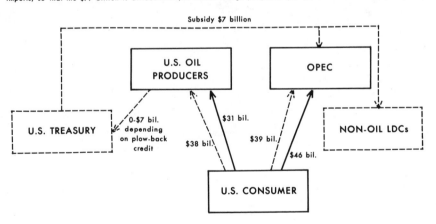

a) If reinvestment is high, Treasury gets less revenue but the prospect of more U.S. oil.
b) If reinvestment is low, Treasury gets back the subsidy costs and nothing is lost.

Figure 5-1. Illustrative Assumptions

Table 5-2
Payments for U.S. Domestic and Imported Oil, 1976–1983

	Actual			Projected					Average 1979–1983
	1976	1977	1978	1979	1980	1981	1982	1983	
Consumption (billion bbl)	6.2	6.7	6.8	6.9	7.0	7.1	7.2	7.3	7.1
Production, including Alaska (billion bbl)	3.8	3.8	4.0	3.9	3.8	3.9	3.9	4.0	3.9
Imports (billion bbl)	2.4	2.9	2.8	3.0	3.2	3.2	3.3	3.3	3.2
Average prices ($/bbl)									
Foreign	13.00	14.00	14.00	15.50	16.25	17.06	17.95	18.85	17.12
Domestic	8.10	9.00	9.90	11.00	12.00	13.31	14.52	15.97	13.38
Weighted average	10.00	11.16	11.59	12.96	14.00	15.00	16.08	17.27	15.06
Oil payments by U.S. consumer ($ billion)									
Under existing regulations									
Domestic Oil	30.8	34.2	39.6	42.9	46.0	51.9	56.6	63.9	52.2
Foreign Oil	31.2	40.6	39.2	46.5	52.0	54.6	59.2	62.2	54.8
Total	62.0	74.8	78.8	89.4	98.0	106.5	115.8	126.1	107.0
Under proposed plan									
Domestic Oil	38.0	46.4	46.4	50.5	53.2	58.5	62.7	68.1	58.8
Foreign Oil	24.0	32.4	32.4	38.9	44.8	48.0	53.1	57.0	48.2
Total	62.0	74.8	78.8	89.4	98.0	106.5	115.8	126.1	107.0
Payments by U.S. government's to oil exporters ($ billion):	7.2	8.2	6.8	7.6	7.2	6.6	6.1	5.2	6.6
$/bbl import price differentials	3.00	2.84	2.41	2.54	2.25	2.75	1.87	1.58	2.06
$/bbl tax	1.90	2.16	1.69	1.96	1.70	1.79	1.56	1.30	1.68

average over $17 per barrel, up from the 1976 average of $13 per barrel. Under current U.S. regulations, U.S. crude-oil prices will increase at a rate of about 10 percent per year over the 1979–1983 period, averaging close to $13.40 per barrel—some $5.30 above the average crude-oil price in 1976.

Using the proportions of domestic production versus imports implied in these projections, the weighted average cost of crude oil to the U.S. consumer over the five-year period has been projected. This average crude-oil price in the U.S. (made up of the composite domestic price and the delivered price of foreign oil) is likely to rise by about 7 percent per year to 1980 and to average $15.06 per barrel, up over $5 from the $10.00 per barrel paid in 1976.

At these projected volumes and prices over the 1979–1983 period, U.S. oil consumers would spend an average of $107 billion per year for both foreign and domestic oil. On average, 49 percent of these payments would go to domestic crude-oil producers, while 51 percent would be paid to foreign oil-producing countries.

Supposing that the U.S. government were to adopt the proposal outlined in table 5–2. The Treasury would on average pay foreign oil-producing governments directly some $6.6 billion per year, or $2.06 per barrel on average annual imports of 3.2 billion barrels (figures 5–2 and 5–3). There are several options for method of payment—in some cases, an OPEC government might demand cash, and in some cases, U.S. export credits might be negotiated. With some OPEC countries (such as Saudi Arabia and Kuwait) there should be a possibility of selling them long-term U.S. Treasury notes, which would be similar to their purchasing these notes directly. Finally, a portion of these funds might be set aside to help less developed countries alleviate their balance-of-payments deficits. All these options could be negotiated with each OPEC country individually, depending on their particular economic and financial requirements.

As a result of these Treasury payments, the price of foreign oil in the United States would decline to an average of $15.06 per barrel over the four-year period, instead of an average of $17.21 expected under the current system. At the same time, the U.S. government should remove all price controls on domestic oil. The competitive crude-oil market in the United States would rapidly move to the ceiling price set by the cost of imported oil. Some companies that now enjoy very high prices for newly discovered oil might experience some declines in these prices. Many more companies, however, with currently lower-tier oil prices, would experience rapid increases in their average prices. Over the five years U.S. oil companies would gain an average of $1.68 per barrel, although it would be a declining amount as time progressed (see table 5–2). An extra-profits tax, coupled with a "plow-back" credit, should be instituted, so that oil companies will not earn the larger profits from the price decontrol unless they reinvest

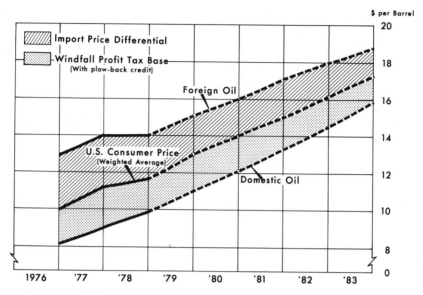

Figure 5-2. Crude-Oil Prices: Comparison of Current Regulations with Proposed Plan

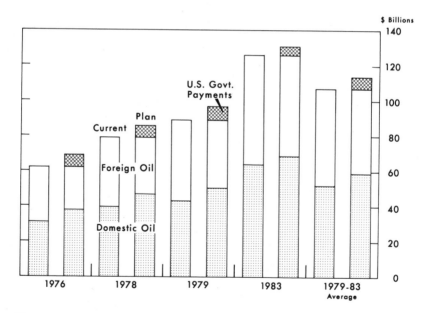

Figure 5-3. The Flow of U.S. Oil Payments: Comparison of Current Regulations with Proposed Plan

those funds in new domestic drilling. Not only will these higher prices induce more drilling in new areas, but more significantly there is likely to be a rapid increase in the pace and depth of drilling around known reservoirs and a higher rate of enhanced oil recovery applications. Shut-in fields, where producers are waiting for prices higher than the current ceilings on old oil, would be rapidly opened up. The extra-profits tax and plow-back credit would be a powerful device for reinvestment, especially for smaller and medium-sized companies. Lifting all price controls on domestic oil could cause a significant increase in U.S. oil production over the next decade.

Because of the payments by the U.S. Treasury to the oil-exporting countries, there would be no increase in the direct cost of oil to the U.S. consumer. If for reasons of conservation or as a result of higher OPEC pricing the U.S. government determines that the U.S. consumer should pay more, the magnitude of the import price differential could be varied. If, for example, OPEC raises prices rapidly, the U.S. government would have the option of raising its import price differential or of allowing U.S. prices to rise by not subsidizing the full amount of the OPEC increase. At the same time, the domestic profits tax would either make up for the U.S. Treasury's foreign payments in the case of only a modest increase in U.S. drilling, or the plow-back credit would buy the nation the prospect of more domestic oil. Because the Treasury will control the import price differential and the taxation of domestic profits, it would be difficult for a company to avoid the extra-profits tax, unless it made the appropriate investments to qualify for the plow-back credit.

A New Fund for Developing Countries

Under the plan proposed here the U.S. Treasury would be paying oil-producing countries over $6.5 billion per year. It would seem appropriate that a portion of these funds should be devoted to helping many of the developing countries out of their balance-of-payments problems, which have been caused in part by the high price of oil. Since these funds would be paid by the U.S. government to OPEC governments in partial payment for oil, it would in effect mean combining a moderately lower price of foreign oil in the U.S. with a commitment by the U.S. to increased development aid. OPEC cooperation in this effort would be needed—if not by all OPEC governments, then at least by those who can afford it.

The North-South dialogue would be a useful forum in which to begin these discussions. Until now the United States has resisted many of the OPEC and developing country proposals concerning a "new international economic order". However, there seems to be some sentiment in the Carter administration toward limited acceptance of the new ideas being proposed by the developing countries. In particular, a massive Common Fund has been proposed for the stabilization of international commodity prices. Acceptance of this plan by the United States would mean the acceptance of generally higher prices for imported raw materials for the United States, which will add to domestic inflationary pressures. The United States should receive something in return for supporting the Common Fund proposal. With the cooperation of some OPEC members, U.S. acceptance of the Common Fund might be linked to financing the associated Common Fund commodity buffer stocks through the U.S. Treasury payments for oil suggested here. In addition, U.S. support for other development proposals, such as the transfer of technology to developing countries or a new worldwide agricultural investment fund, could be tied to OPEC acceptance of using a portion of the Treasury oil payments to finance such schemes. In that way, both the United States and OPEC, as well as any other interested developed countries, could work simultaneously toward a lessening of oil price pressures and toward alleviating some of the economic difficulties of the non-oil developing countries.

The strictly U.S.-OPEC oil-related aspects of the plan proposed here can be kept separate from the developing country aspects—one does not depend on the other. The U.S. Treasury could simply make the oil payments directly to OPEC regardless of what happened in the North-South dialogue. Nevertheless, a diplomatic effort by the United States within that forum could seek an answer from some OPEC governments on the extent to which they are willing to give up at least a portion of their oil-related economic rents to help their brethren in the Third World.

Benefits and Costs

I am proposing a major change in the way in which the U.S. government regulates both the international oil trade and the domestic oil business. Most of the parties affected should benefit from the change:

The U.S. consumer would continue to be as protected from high-priced OPEC oil as he is now under the present control system.

The domestic oil industry would be relieved of the heavy burden of the current regulatory system that encourages imports of foreign oil and discourages production of domestic oil.

If certain OPEC governments would accept U.S. Treasury notes, U.S. balance-of-payments pressures would be reduced.

The U.S. government would become a more active participant in the highly political arena of international oil.

With OPEC cooperation the non-oil developing countries could be helped by increased development aid and by possible U.S. support for a number of their recent proposals.

Perhaps most important, the United States would significantly enhance its prospects for increasing its oil production, which is clearly at the heart of much of the energy policy controversy.

There are, nevertheless, a number of political and economic costs that must be weighed against these benefits. First, the international oil companies have urged the U.S. government not to become involved in oil-related negotiations with the OPEC governments. The companies have argued that U.S. government involvement would introduce complicating political forces into the bargaining process, limiting the commercial flexibility of the companies and potentially impeding the smooth flow of oil imports into the United States. Although this argument might have had some merit in the past, an opposing point of view suggests that petroleum supplies and prices play such a dominant role in the world today that the U.S. government has an obligation to maintain the military and economic security of the nation through increased involvement in international oil negotiations. This difference of opinion depends primarily on political perspective and can be decided only by the elected members of the U.S. government.

A second objection to this policy recommendation could come from those who would view U.S. government payments to OPEC as a misuse of public funds, in lending a further degree of legitimacy to the oil cartel. While the underlying emotional reasons for this objection are understandable, it is a fact that the international oil companies collect the taxes for OPEC. The only fact this proposal would change is that a portion of this tax collection and its ultimate payment to OPEC would be shifted to the U.S. government, offering possible additional leverage to precisely those who might voice the strongest objections.

The proposed plan would impose an added administrative burden on the U.S. government. An apparatus for administering an oil import quota, as well as some additional means of monitoring the possible re-export of the lower-priced imported oil, would have to be set up. On the other hand, the domestic regulatory apparatus could be shrunk significantly, so that there would probably be a net decrease in overall oil industry regulatory costs and administrative burdens.

The underlying economic cost of this proposal is the potential increase in the federal budget deficit. If the U.S. government could convince certain OPEC governments to purchase government securities with the import subsidy payments, the increase in the federal deficit would be automatically financed and to that extent would not cause additional inflationary or interest rate pressures. Where some increases in tax revenues from domestic oil companies would come about from the extra-profits tax, there would be some additional offset to the increase in the budget deficit. To the extent that the plan would increase the federal budget deficit, however, the U.S. oil companies would be increasing their domestic drilling expenditures, offering the United States the prospect of more domestic energy supplies. In a sense, therefore, the increased deficit could be viewed as an additional public investment in energy security, and a probably less expensive investment than the strategic petroleum reserve.

A final objection relates to the possible reduced domestic price of new oil the companies would receive under this proposal. Although the average price of U.S. oil would increase, there could be a moderate decline in upper-tier new oil prices. This decrease, however, would be more than offset by increases in prices of oil produced from older wells, so that on balance oil company revenues would increase. To take advantage of the plow-back credit contemplated as part of the extra-profits tax, it seems likely that most oil companies would increase their drilling both in new and existing oil fields. Under current regulations new oil is priced at about $13 per barrel and is scheduled to rise to about $16 per barrel by 1983. Under this plan new oil would average about $15 per barrel over the same period, only slightly less than is likely under current regulations.

Conclusions

The principal objectives of government energy policy, within the limits of the immediate technical and political constraints, appear to be to achieve the greatest possible self-reliance from unreliable and monopoly-priced foreign oil sources, and to prevent energy shortages from causing increasing economic dislocations.

There are two separate sets of issues associated with the energy crisis. The first is an international problem, affecting U.S. foreign political and economic policies. These problems relate to OPEC control of world oil supplies, which represents a fundamental change in the world power structure. The second is a domestic economic problem related to a changing set of social values among decision makers in the United States. Present energy policies have so confused these two sets of issues that neither objective is being met—the United States is further away from achieving them than it was in 1973. In particular, increasing constraints on domestic energy production since 1973 have increased the necessity to import oil from OPEC.

The proposal made in this chapter would allow government policy to separate these two aspects of the energy issue and to frame specific programs to deal with each separately. From an international point of view the United States would be in a more favorable position to deal with internal OPEC frictions. On the domestic side, the U.S. crude-oil market would be insulated from foreign pressures, potentially enhancing domestic competition and improving the prospects for increased domestic oil supplies. Finally, the proposal should complement the major government emphasis on coal and conservation. Energy security will ultimately come from a combination of policies, not only from those designed to promote less energy consumption and a greater use of alternate sources but also from a more rational regulatory approach to the petroleum aspects of the total energy problem.

Notes

1. U.S. Department of the Treasury, *The OPEC Price Increases: Impact on the United States Economy,* January 1977.

The Case for an Import Quota: No Self-Embargo Needed

M.A. Adelman of the Massachusetts Institute of Technology advocates the adoption of a bidding system for U.S. oil imports. He suggests that the U.S. government estimate our oil import needs and then use an auction technique to apportion that amount among would-be suppliers of imported oil. The competitive bidding for the right to sell this clearly defined quantity of oil would put each supplier under pressure to sell at a lower price in order to gain access to a larger share of the U.S. market. In the present surplus state of the oil market, this approach has an appreciable prospect for achieving success.

The U.S. should exempt Canada and Mexico from the oil import quota and encourage a North American free-trade zone in oil and gas.

Over the next several years it is likely that the United States may again impose a quota on imported oil. While this response to growing oil imports may not be the most efficient policy from an economic point of view, it could be the most acceptable policy from a political point of view.

There are a number of distinct and growing pressures pointing toward an oil import quota. First, there is little prospect that a crude-oil equalization tax will ever pass the Congress. As a result, the original centerpiece of the administration's proposed energy plan will have to be replaced by either a quota or a tariff on oil imports. The tariff option, at first sight the more reasonable, faces two problems. Congressional resistance to higher oil prices on inflationary grounds suggests that oil import fees will not be accepted. Total decontrol of crude-oil prices would clearly be the best option, but this is even less likely than the crude-oil tax. Second, the present entitlements system could tend to make the tariff work in a perverse manner. That is, with the present entitlement paid by refiners of domestic oil to refiners of imported oil, domestic production is discouraged while foreign imports are encouraged. A fee on imported oil could seriously exacerbate this behavior, by substantially increasing the value of the entitlement.

If a tariff were imposed to fully supplement any proposed wellhead tax on domestic oil, the tariff on imports would have to be about $5 per barrel. In other words, foreign crude oil would then cost importing refiners $20 per barrel, versus $10 per barrel for domestic oil. This wide margin would mean substantially larger entitlements payments, causing a greater use of imported oil, as refiners using imported crude oil strive to maximize their entitlements payments by increasing their use of foreign oil. As a result, a tariff would probably have the perverse effect of increasing imports even if it did reduce domestic oil consumption somewhat. The quota may be the only feasible alternative to the now defunct domestic crude-oil well-head tax.

The second set of pressures for an oil import quota comes from those who argue that the only way to achieve conservation is through the imposition of a fixed limit on oil imports: If this means that domestic oil prices rise, so be it! Or, some would argue, a rationing system should be imposed. In any event, there is strong sentiment in some quarters for a kind of self-embargo, as the only way to stop our growing dependence on foreign oil.

Third, a quota may eventually be needed to keep out cheap, foreign oil. As strange as this seems, it has in fact occurred in some petroleum product markets. Because of excess refining capacity in large efficient overseas refineries, some petroleum products can be manufactured and delivered to the United States at a price lower than that needed by some domestic refiners to stay profitable. More important, as the cost of U.S. crude oil rises relative to foreign oil prices over the next few years, we may see the emergence of political pressure by domestic producers to reimpose a crude-oil quota.

Finally, a quota would be the first step in implementing one of a number of plans designed to dilute some of OPEC's price-setting powers in the world oil market. The sealed bid auction system, for example, requires the imposition of a variable import quota. Once the quota is established, the method of allocation could become a powerful tool in the hands of the U.S. government to influence world oil prices.

The impact of a quota on foreign exchange markets is likely to be positive. Foreign holders of dollars, now deeply concerned over the lack of a U.S. energy policy to stem the growing dollar outflow, would know immediately the maximum amount that the United States would import. As a result, concern over an increasing flood of dollars overseas would be lessened and the dollar's value should improve in the foreign exchange market.

OPEC and Oil Company Reactions

The plan outlined in chapter 5 is not intended to break up OPEC, and the OPEC governments should not react negatively to it. The purpose of the plan is to achieve a greater rate of U.S. oil production while continuing to balance equity versus efficiency in the price of oil to the U.S. consumer.

In the past the oil import quota was designed to prevent lower-priced foreign oil from entering the United States in volumes sufficient to impair the domestic oil industry. U.S. crude oil was ample to satisfy much of the U.S. market. During 1972 the import quota program was abolished. A year later OPEC had almost total control of the world's oil markets. With the vastly increased importing of foreign oil in the past several years, renewal of an import quota system may now be appropriate. The U.S. government has a vital interest in the magnitude, price, and source of foreign oil. Under my plan the U.S. government would play a major role in subsidizing that foreign oil, so that U.S. companies could deliver it to the U.S. market at lower prices. To prevent some companies from taking advantage of the subsidy, some limits will have to be placed on U.S. oil imports. An import quota would also permit a more flexible policy in determining the appropriate value for the import price differential as market conditions change over time. The imposition of a variable import quota, to be administered in combination with the government-to-government import price differential, would be a powerful tool in the hands of the U.S. government, both in influencing the international oil companies in the pattern of their oil imports and in negotiations with OPEC governments. If, for example, a particular OPEC government decided to sell more oil to the United States, both the magnitude of the import price differential and the amount of that additional oil would be determined in part by U.S. government policy.

It is true that this plan would alter some of the existing arrangements between the international oil companies and the OPEC governments. Nevertheless, oil is a highly political commodity today, and it is the responsibility of the U.S. government to set foreign policy, be it political or economic. The international companies would still retain their major technical roles, but the price at which they purchase oil from OPEC governments would be determined in part by the U.S. government.

While the international companies would be losing some control overseas, they would be gaining an essentially free oil market in the United States. Their incentives for drilling in the United States would be increased, and they would be less subject to criticism of their international relationships. Some primarily domestic refining companies, now wedded to the entitlements system, might have to give up their windfalls, but these derive from bad regulations anyway.

Nature of the Quota

How large a quota should the United States set? How should the quota be distributed between crude oil and petroleum products? What other special relationships might the United States want to encourage through special exemptions from the quota? While detailed answers to these and related questions cannot be definitely settled in these few pages, some initial responses can be sketched.

First, the United States today imports 2.0 million to 2.5 million barrels per day (MMB/D) of refined products in addition to the 6.0 to 6.5 MMB/D of crude oil. About half of these refined product imports represent heavy fuel oils from Venezuela and the Caribbean, a long-established trade between the utilities and industries of the Northeast and the oil companies who originally built the refining complexes in these foreign areas. If this market were exempted from quota, it is doubtful that any major switching would occur, since the profitability of the product is limited and transport costs from other parts of the world with sufficient refining capacity would be prohibitive. Under the assumption that Venezuelan and Caribbean heavy fuel oils were exempt from quota, this leaves 1.0 to 1.5 MMB/D of other refined product imports. In the interest of encouraging the construction of more U.S. refining capacity, it would seem that these product imports, refined largely from Mideast and African crude oils, should be subject to quota restrictions. I would advocate a gradually declining percentage of some base-period import levels as a reasonable compromise between the conflicting interests that are bound to arise in this area. These percentages should be announced for several years in advance, leaving ample time for new U.S. refining capacity to be built to replace the declining petroleum product imports.

The import quota for crude oil should be neither so low as to create a self-embargo nor so high as to permit the displacement of U.S. or other exempt crude oils. An optimistic forecast of a fairly level import requirement for the next five years would mean an average annual crude-oil import figure of 2.2 to 2.4 billion barrels (6.0 to 6.5 MMB/D). During some months the average daily figure could be higher but would have to be offset by lower imports in other months.

Table 6-1 shows a wide variation in the potential crude-oil imports by 1983. The purpose of the quota would be to hold down the increase in crude-oil imports as much as possible. If the optimistic U.S. supply scenario were to develop, then quota limits would not be reached, and market price competition would prevail. On the other hand, if the pessimistic U.S. supply scenario were to develop, required crude imports could be as high as 11.5 MMB/D, some 5 MMB/D higher than the proposed quota. There are two complementary approaches for dealing with this pessimistic U.S. supply scenario. The first relates to the allocation and pricing of those crude-oil imports that would be permitted under the quota. The next section will discuss this option in the light of M.A. Adelman's sealed bidding approach. The other complementary alternative would be to exempt all North American crude oil (Mexican and Canadian) from the quota. Rapidly growing

Table 6-1
Alternative U.S. Import Cases for 1983
(in millions of barrels per day)

| | | Forecasted Scenario, 1983 | |
	Estimated, 1978	*Optimistic*	*Pessimistic*
Demand[a]	19.0	20.0	22.0
U.S. supplies[b]	11.0	12.0	9.0
Product imports[c]	2.0	1.5	1.5
Required crude-oil imports	6.0	6.5	11.5

[a] Excludes strategic reserve.
[b] Includes all hydrocarbon feedstocks, from the lower forty-eight states and Alaska.
[c] Assumes declining product imports.

Mexican crude-oil production will need to find new markets. On the basis of transportation costs alone, this Mexican crude oil should be able to displace Mideast and African crude oils in the U.S. Gulf Coast and the Caribbean refining centers. This transition should be encouraged by the U.S. government. It is important that any crude-oil quota exempt Mexican oil and, to the extent that the Canadians desire it, also exempt Canadian crude oil. This exemption would stimulate price competition in the international crude-oil market, in particular for that oil coming in under the quota. That is, the 6.0 to 6.5 MMB/D of quota oil would still have to compete with Mexican and Canadian crude oils. To the extent that the United States required greater quantities of foreign crude oil, these increments could come largely from Mexico.

The Adelman Plan

My proposal to couple the decontrol of U.S. crude-oil prices with the imposition of a quota on foreign oil and U.S. government determination of the price of foreign oil in the United States is related to M.A. Adelman's sealed-bid proposal. Once the quota on crude oil is imposed, some method of allocation will be required. The old U.S. import quota (1958-1972) used historical refinery runs as a basis for this allocation. In the face of lower foreign oil prices historically, this import license had a positive value. Today, with higher foreign oil prices and the entitlements system, it is difficult to predict what would happen to the value of an import license under a quota system.

Under my plan the United States could set a firm price ceiling of $15 per barrel for all crude oil sold in the United States, both foreign and domestic, from 1979–1983. All crude oil imported into the United States (except for Mexican and Canadian) would be subject to the quota and to the proposed bidding system. That bid could be positive; a selling entity could pay the U.S. government for the right to sell its oil in the United States. Or that bid could be negative; a selling entity could require payment from the U.S. government over and above the $15 per barrel delivered price. In this latter case the U.S. government would determine on the basis of all bids whether to pay this negative bid (the import price differential proposed in chapter 5). In order for this approach to be effective, U.S. domestic oil would have to be decontrolled, that is, priced at the same ceiling as foreign oil. This would encourage maximum growth of domestic supplies and put a ceiling on the quantity of imports, with exempted Mexican and Canadian oil treated essentially as domestic. Since Mexican oil is not produced by any of the major international oil companies, arm's-length bargaining between purchasing refiner and crude-oil seller will be assured.

While this proposed system appears complex, it is in reality far less complicated than the present system of domestic regulation. With a fixed U.S. price ceiling on all oil, foreign and domestic, at a level commensurate with present costs, this plan will leave consumers at least as well off as they are under present regulations, and potentially better off. The proposed ceiling, on the other hand, is high enough to satisfy most producer interests, at least in the United States. By accepting bids on quota oil above or below the ceiling, the U.S. would be stimulating competition among the OPEC countries for the now large U.S. market. Finally, the maximum encouragement would be given for Mexican oil to enter the U.S. market.

Figure 6–1 depicts in principle what is being proposed. OPEC country A decides that it wishes to receive $15.00 per barrel for its oil. Transport costs are assumed at $1.50 per barrel, so the delivered price to the United States is $16.50, $1.50 above the ceiling price. This bid is submitted to the U.S. government, with a request for payment to it of an additional $1.50 per barrel. OPEC country B, because it desires to sell more oil, requests only $13.50 per barrel, so that with $1.50 transport, the U.S. delivered price is $15.00 per barrel; thus no government payment is required. OPEC country C is really anxious to sell more oil, so it reduces its bid to $12.00 per barrel, plus $1.50 transport. Since the oil will sell for $15.00 per barrel, OPEC country C is paying the U.S. government $1.50 per barrel for the right to sell its oil in the United States. All these OPEC countries are competing for the U.S. quota oil market. At the same time, Mexico, with a much lower transport cost, can sell as much oil as it desires in the United States, subject

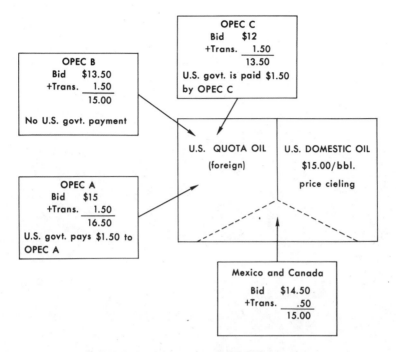

Figure 6-1. Competing OPEC Countries

only to the price established by competitive U.S. market forces. With a coming international surplus of crude oil, this system could dilute a large measure of OPEC's price-setting power and enable the United States to determine at least in part how much it should pay for crude oil.

7

The Foreign Tax Credit

The present system of foreign tax credits under certain circumstances may help link the interests of some international companies with those of some OPEC members. As a general proposition the companies should be encouraged to bargain for crude oil at arm's length, thereby promoting competition among the OPEC states for world markets. The present system of foreign tax credits for certain crude–oil purchases may not be helpful in achieving that objective.

In the past four years there have been at least two major congressional inquiries into the use of foreign tax credits by international oil companies. The first set of hearings was conducted in 1975 under the aegis of the Foreign Economic Policy subcommittee of the Senate Foreign Relations Committee. More recently, during the fall of 1977, a subcommittee of the Government Operations Committee of the House of Representatives probed more deeply into the issue. The fundamental premise of both congressional investigations was that misuse of foreign tax credits by some international oil companies is costing the U.S. taxpayer substantial amounts of money, is serving to maintain OPEC's monopolistic pricing structure, and is discouraging those oil companies from more intensive oil exploration outside the OPEC countries.

This alleged collusion between certain international oil companies and some key OPEC member states may be an important peg on which OPEC's cohesion rests. OPEC differs from the classic cartel in several important respects, not the least of which is the dominant role of Saudi Arabia. To what extent does the "creditability" of Saudi Arabian taxes by certain American oil companies against their U.S. tax liabilities tie these companies to producing Saudi oil rather than oil from other sources? To a lesser degree similar questions can be raised concerning oil produced from several other OPEC countries. To understand the nature of this linkage and the role of the foreign tax credit in strengthening that linkage, one must probe further into just how the OPEC cartel actually functions.

First, the OPEC cartel has never set the volume of oil to be produced among its member states. That quantity is always left up to each individual member country, and that decision is usually taken in conjunction with the major oil companies who physically take the oil out of the ground and out of the exporting country. That is, as a seller the individual OPEC member state must reach agreement with the purchasing oil companies about the volume of oil production. It has typically been the buying companies who have determined the volumes coming out of each OPEC member country. Thus the companies have considerable leverage in determining how much oil each OPEC member will produce.

Second, the manner in which OPEC has succeeded in controlling world oil prices is related to the creditability of foreign oil taxes by American firms. In particular, OPEC as a group establishes an average revenue per barrel for the marker crude—Saudi Arabian light, FOB the Persian Gulf. This OPEC government take permits member states to enjoy considerable flexibility on the means of achieving it, through taxation, royalties, production-sharing agreements, or other means depending on relations between the individual OPEC governments and the oil companies operating in that country. The individual OPEC government, in seeking to maximize its revenues, works with the purchasing oil companies in structuring an appropriate formula to minimize the taxes that these companies will have to pay to the U.S. Treasury and to the governments of other consuming countries. That is where the issue of foreign tax credits arises and is at least one of the reasons why some international oil companies have become so dependent on OPEC oil.

Historical Background

The current tax credit treatment originated in the early 1950s. At that time Saudi Arabia decided to seek more revenues from its oil properties, through the imposition of income taxes on Aramco (the Arabian–American Oil Company, which produces most of the oil in Saudi Arabia). The oil companies, which owned and managed Aramco, had so structured their accounting procedures that Aramco showed no profit, because the transfer price of crude oil from Aramco to the oil companies' refining and marketing subsidiaries was kept artificially low. By the early 1950s the government of Saudi Arabia decided that it would set the posted price of crude oil, regardless of what product prices might be in the consumer markets. The tax on Aramco would be based on posted prices, set at a level at which Aramco would make a profit and thereby have taxable income for the government of Saudi Arabia. The response of the oil companies was to work with the Saudi Arabian government to structure the arrangement so that the real impact of the Saudi tax would be borne by taxpayers in the consuming country rather than by company profits. The device used was the foreign tax credit, a ruling by the U.S. Treasury that the companies would not have to pay income tax to two different governments on the same income. (The Treasury had issued a similar ruling in 1950 regarding oil taxes paid to the Venezuelan government.) Thus any taxes paid by Aramco to Saudi Arabia became creditable against the U.S. tax liabilities of the oil companies. Other oil-producing countries quickly followed the Saudi lead.

During the fifteen-year period 1955-1970, the differential between market prices and posted prices inceased. An overabundance of oil supplies kept market prices relatively low, while posted prices were forced upward by the Saudi desire for more tax revenues. Oil company payments to producing countries became increasingly based on the posted price, artificially set without regard to market forces, without regard to actual profit or loss on the sale of a barrel of oil. As the producing countries received a higher tax based on these artificial posted prices, the oil companies received increasing tax credits to wipe out their tax liabilities on other operations, primarily in the United States.

In the early 1970s the governments of the oil-producing countries began to negotiate for control of the oil concessions, that is, full ownership of their oil resources. The oil companies did not want a cash payment for the full value of the concession because it would be subject to large capital gains taxes. As a result, the concept of "buyback" oil was created, in which the former concession owners would purchase oil from the host government at a price below the world market. The profit made on the resale of this buyback oil would be treated as compensation but would be tax-free to the companies because of the credits that had piled up from the basic tax payments.

During 1975, after most of the oil concessions had been totally or partially nationalized, the oil companies created the concept of a service fee for the provision of petroleum-related services to the host government. This service fee is booked as foreign income and is fully creditable against prior tax credits. Net of Saudi taxes, this fee is worth $0.80 per barrel and gives the Aramco partners both a price advantage over other competitors and continued exemption from the capital gains tax. It is significant that the Saudi's have not yet fully taken over Aramco and retain only 60 percent ownership. The remaining 40 percent continues to permit the companies to use the foreign tax credit.

How It Works

The starting point in the tax computation is a completely arbitrary figure, having no connection with profit or loss from the sale of oil. It is not really a tax on income but rather a royalty or economic rent charged by the producing country. Table 7-1 illustrates the Saudi Arabian tax in 1975.

As a result of this "income" tax, American companies operating in

Table 7–1
Illustration of OPEC Tax Computation: 1975
(in dollars per barrel)

Posted price		$11.25
Less: Royalty (20 percent)	$2.25	
Production cost	.12	
	2.37	
Tax base		9.88
"Income" tax (85 percent)		7.55
Government take (tax and royalty)		9.80

Source: Foreign Tax Credits Claimed By U.S. Petroleum Companies, U.S. House of Representatives, Government Operations Committee; testimony of Dr. Laurence Woodward, Assistant Secretary for Tax Policy, U.S. Treasury Department; Oct. 1977, p.260.

Saudi Arabia claimed a foreign tax credit of $7.55 per barrel on most of the oil that they exported from the country. This was a tax credit against the taxes that they owed the U.S. government from their earnings in the United States and in other countries. Table 7–2 shows the magnitude of these credits in 1975.

In 1975, therefore, for all U.S. oil companies operating overseas, the foreign tax credit came to almost $15 billion, reducing their taxes from almost $18 billion to less than $2.5 billion. Suppose that the companies were required to treat their tax payments to the OPEC governments as royalties, or business expenses, which would be deductible from their gross receipts rather than creditable against their U.S. taxes. Then in 1975 they would have reported about $17 billion in foreign taxable income ($31.9 less $14.8 billion, table 7–2), so that their U.S. tax liability on foreign income would have been about $8.5 billion. Coupled with the $2 billion that they owed on domestic income, they would have paid $10.5 billion in taxes rather than the $2.5 billion that they actually paid.

This argument is faulty, however, because the foreign tax cannot exceed 48 percent of foreign taxable income. Thus the $14.8 billion shown in table 7–2 represents a ceiling on the amount of creditable foreign taxes. Had the companies been required to take a deduction instead of a credit they could have reduced their foreign taxable income by as much as 95 percent. In most OPEC countries the combination of high posted prices and the very high OPEC taxes would have meant an effective foreign tax rate on actual income of around 95 percent. To understand this, one must refer to the posted price of $11.25 shown in table 7–1. This price was about 7 percent above the so-called market price in 1975. Thus the companies received only $10.47 per barrel for their oil exports from Saudi Arabia, against

Table 7–2
U.S. Tax Liability of U.S. Oil Companies, 1975
(in billions of dollars)

	Domestic	Foreign	Total
Taxable income	6.6	31.9	38.5
Tax liabilities without foreign tax credits	2.5	15.3	17.8
Tax credits			
Foreign tax credits	—	14.8	14.8
Domestic tax credits	0.6	—	0.6
Tax liabilities with foreign tax credits	1.9	0.5	2.4

Source: Foreign Tax Credits Claimed By U.S. Petroleum Companies, U.S. House of Representatives, Government Operations Committee; testimony of Dr. Laurence Woodward, Assistant Secretary for Tax Policy, U.S. Treasury Department; Oct. 1977, p. 260.

which they paid the Saudi government $9.80 per barrel. The additional $0.12 of per barrel production costs left the companies with only about $0.55 per barrel, or roughly 5 percent of their gross receipts of $10.47 per barrel. As a result, the $31.9 billion in table 7-2 would have been reduced to only $1.5 billion, against which the companies would have paid a 48 percent U.S. tax, or $700 million.

Using this logic the U.S. Treasury has made estimates of the increased U.S. tax liability if foreign oil taxes were deducted instead of credited. Since 1974 the difference in taxes paid to the U.S. government would have been in the range of $1 billion to $2 billion annually for American companies operating in OPEC countries.[1] While one could question the method of computation used in determining this figure, the conclusion seems to be that the companies are not really taking unfair advantage of the U.S. tax laws, and the U.S. taxpayer is not subsidizing OPEC, at least not from the foreign tax credit viewpoint. Since U.S. government receipts are about $500 billion per year, the extra $1 billion to $2 billion that the companies are gaining at the expense of the U.S. taxpayer would hardly matter in the overall federal budget. It has even been argued that denying the credit to U.S. companies would subject them to higher tax burdens than their foreign competitors.

Nevertheless, the annual after-tax earnings for those U.S. oil companies with substantial operations in OPEC countries are in the range of $6 billion to $7 billion. Thus the additional $1 billion to $2 billion of aftertax earnings resulting from the creditability of foreign taxes has become quite significant to those companies. Alteration of the system of foreign tax credits could, therefore, substantially change the behavior of those few companies in their dealings with OPEC.

The Real Issue

If the sums forgone by the U.S. Treasury are not sizable, and if eliminating the foreign tax credit would put U.S. companies at a competitive disadvantage, why then have many astute observers in Washington stressed this issue so frequently and so adamantly? The answer may be partly emotional and partly real.

The emotional criticism seems to stem from an acute sense of frustration concerning the institutional rigidities contributing to the continued strength of OPEC and a resulting distrust of the major oil companies. Presumption of wrongdoing, no matter how ill founded, will continue to plague the oil industry until these frustrations are overcome.

The sharp rise in the price of oil in late 1973 and during 1974 as mandated by OPEC is perceived to be a threat to the stability of the Western economies or at least a critical loss of control by the governments of these countries over their economic destinies. What seems to rankle the American public and therefore the U.S. Congress is that we have lost control over the pricing and production of so vital a commodity as oil. In the absence of making the hard choices to attain a greater degree of energy self-reliance, the response of frustration is to attack the symbol of oil wealth and power: the major oil companies.

If it is this frustration that is causing the emotional outburst against "big oil," then the major oil companies have not helped alleviate the confrontation. The oil industry keeps telling the American public that there is no way it can break loose from the cartel's control, at least not in the near future. Despite the advent of the Alaskan pipeline, the rapidly growing production from the North Sea and Mexico, and solid production gains in other parts of the world, the industry maintains that we will be heavily dependent on OPEC oil for many years to come. Despite the fact that OPEC now has excess capacity of somewhere between 10 million and 12 million barrels per day—that is, 25%-30% of its producing capability is unused—very little price weakness has emerged in the oil markets. In the minds of many Americans this suggests not only the cohesion of OPEC but also the possible cooperation of certain major oil companies with the cartel. After all, these companies work at least indirectly for the OPEC cartel and actually manage the transportation, processing, and eventual sale of the oil for the OPEC governments. While the oil industry steadfastly maintains that it has little power to negotiate with the OPEC governments, the oil companies make their profits from producing crude oil in the OPEC countries to satisfy markets in the West, which only they can supply in the major quantities required.

This is not meant to suggest that the industry is involved with the cartel because of insidious motives. It simply reflects the fact that each company's profits are directly tied to a unique supply and transportation system that makes them dependent on the OPEC governments in terms of pricing. The volume of production in a given country is still determined chiefly by what each company thinks it can ultimately sell in the world market.

As the public's suspicions grow, the industry continues to rail against interference from Washington. As valid as some of the oil companies' complaints may be, the underlying congressional perception persists that the major oil companies are not doing enough to combat the cartel in the interests of the American public. The Senate Subcommittee on Multinational Corporations put it this way:

> The ability of OPEC to reduce its production and hold or raise its revenue levels will rest upon its ability to prorate production cutbacks satisfactorily among its member countries. This prorationing capability is enhanced by the common interest shared by the oil companies and the oil producing countries. First, access to crude oil is the necessary precondition for an oil company to stay in business. In a supply-limited situation, a refiner without secure access to crude is faced with the high probability of being unable to operate. Second, the price at which OPEC sells oil to companies other than the traditional concessionaries has, up to this time at least, been somewhat higher than the cost of similar oil to the established majors. *Finally, certain tax advantages which reduce the real cost of oil accrue to a company from its ownership of equity oil in a foreign producer country. Thus, for example, a company which lifts part of its foreign oil at tax-paid cost may presently credit the income tax portion of that cost against its U.S. tax liability on other foreign income (italics added).*

> The multinational oil companies, on the other hand, provide OPEC with important advantages. As vertically integrated corporations, the major oil companies guarantee OPEC members an assured outlet for their production in world markets. The primary concern of the established major oil companies is to maintain their world market shares and their favored position of receiving oil from OPEC nations at costs slightly lower than other companies. To maintain this favored status, the international companies help proration production cutbacks among the OPEC members. Their ability to do this derives from the existence of their diversified production base in OPEC countries.

> Thus the current changeover from the concession system to exclusive long-term, large volume supply contracts does not alter the interest that the international oil companies have in helping OPEC carry out its production and pricing policies. So long as the individual OPEC countries have assured outlets for their oil through exclusive joint arrangements with the major oil companies, the divisions within OPEC are unlikely to manifest themselves in lower oil prices, even in the face of a worldwide surplus of

crude oil productive capacity. There are thus parallel interests between OPEC and the major oil companies in which the companies ensure their access to the crude but at the price imposed by OPEC regardless of a theoretical crude oil surplus.[2]

Powerless to alter these international relationships, serious congressional critics of the oil industry have turned to areas where U.S. regulations can be applied. Whether this severe congressional criticism of the international industry is justified or not, the perception of a symbiotic relationship between the major oil companies and the governments of the oil-exporting countries firmly exists in certain influential Washington circles. As a result, the desire to alter the system of foreign tax credits represents an attempt to dilute the international preferred access of the major oil companies.

To understand the concept of preferred access, one has to look a bit more closely at the economic aspects of oil production and the structure of the international petroleum market. By its nature, the oil industry has a built-in propensity to overproduction. Since it is heavily capital intensive, overhead costs are high, while operating expenses are relatively light. As a result, the cost of producing the incremental barrel (marginal cost, to the economist) is low, generally no more than $0.50 in most Middle Eastern oil fields. When there are many producers competing for business, there is a tendency to cut prices and flood the market. Disorderly marketing and wasteful overproduction had been avoided during most of the postwar period because the bulk of the international oil trade had been in the hands of integrated oil companies. Each one of these integrated enterprises kept production of its own crude oil in line with the absorptive capacity of its own market outlets. Although some oil did not flow through these integrated channels, the dominance of the vertically integrated international oil companies ensured the orderly expansion of production in line with the steady growth of demand, and this was accomplished at prices that were remarkably low by present OPEC standards.

Both the OPEC oil ministers and the executives of the international oil companies realize the importance of maintaining this integrated structure, despite the transfer of ownership to the governments of the producing countries. From the viewpoint of OPEC the Saudi Arabian oil minister, Sheik Yamani, has succinctly defined the necessity of maintaining a mutuality of interest between OPEC and the international oil companies as follows:

Nationalization of the upstream (production) operations would inevitably deprive the majors (major oil companies) of any further interest in buying the crude from the producing countries and moving it to their markets in Europe, Japan, and the rest of the world. In other words, their present integrated profit structure, whereby the bulk of their profits are concentrated in the producing end, would be totally transformed. With the elimination of their profit margin from production operations, the majors would have to make this up by shifting their profit focus downstream to their refining and product-marketing operations. Consequently their interest would be identical with that of the consumers—namely, to buy crude oil at the cheapest price possible.[3]

This symbiotic relationship between the OPEC governments and the international oil companies is a principal peg on which the oil cartel hangs together. The current changeover from the oil company concession arrangements to exclusive long-term, large-volume supply contracts between the OPEC governments and international oil companies does not alter this mutually profitable interdependence. So long as the individual OPEC countries have assured outlets for their oil through exclusive arrangements with major oil companies, the natural divisions among the member states of OPEC are unlikely to manifest themselves in lower oil prices, despite a vast worldwide surplus of crude-oil production capacity.

The international oil companies represent the only single cohesive bloc that can to some degree blunt the market power of OPEC. They can, and do from time to time, play off one producing country against another. In a surplus market these companies dictate which OPEC countries will have their oil production cut back, both the volumes of oil and the timing of the oil shipments. Forcing OPEC to make its own decisions regarding the allocation of these cutbacks among its member countries would put a severe strain on the cartel's cohesion.

The interests of the OPEC members are different enough to be susceptible to the conventional process of commercial negotiation. The foreign tax credit system substantially limits the incentives of some major international oil companies to bargain at arm's length over the price of crude oil. This tax preference system is not, therefore, in the interest of the oil-consuming countries. U.S. government policy should be directed to break this link between members of OPEC and the international oil companies. The United States would then have, at least in part, the leverage of the purchasing oil companies working to its advantage, not to the advantage of OPEC.

Recommendations

If the goal of the U.S. government is to dilute the price-setting powers of OPEC, then it would be useful for the government to discourage membership in the organization. For a cartel to work effectively it must have an organization, rules of conduct, and meetings. Although every exporting oil country, OPEC member or not, seeks the highest price in the market, it is the OPEC cartel that controls the market price. As a result, the U.S. government should disallow the foreign tax credit on oil produced in countries that belong to OPEC. It could, on the other hand, permit and even encourage the use of the credit to oil companies producing in non-OPEC countries, thereby increasing the companies incentives to explore for oil there.

There is some precedence for this proposal. The United States today will not grant most-favored-nation status (MFN), which permits countries to export to the United States without having to pay heavy tarrifs and duties on many products, to OPEC member countries. This has angered some in Venezuela but has been effective in discouraging Mexico from seeking to join the cartel. The OPEC versus non-OPEC distinction applied to MFN status could be equally applied in the case of the foreign tax credit.

The congressional hearings conducted by the House Government Operations Committee during the fall of 1977 tended to focus in part on the legal aspects of the foreign tax credit. (See appendix B for a full discussion of the many unresolved legal aspects of the foreign tax credit issue.) Critics of the tax credit system suggested that the abuse was occurring in the definition of income taxes versus royalties imposed by oil-producing countries. As a result, under U.S. tax laws these credits should be disallowed. Other critics of the foreign tax credit system strongly implied that unfair competitive advantage was being given to the major companies who have the capacity to use the credit, thereby harming various other oil companies who do not have such tax advantages. Finally, some critics charged that these tax laws have encouraged U.S. companies to produce abroad to the detriment of production at home, thereby permitting OPEC to extract greater economic rents than they otherwise would have.

While all these arguments have some merit, I believe that the fundamental case against use of the tax credit for oil produced in OPEC countries is even stronger. The system of foreign tax credits has permitted OPEC to extract its monopoly rents from the oil-consuming nations by making some of the major oil companies into their captive, downstream subsidiaries. Disallowing the credit will encourage some of these companies to bargain at arm's length for oil because their profit incentives will be restructured. Instead of putting a profit premium on OPEC oil, a profit penalty will be imposed. This will shift the exploration interest of the companies, at least in part, toward areas of the world where the tax credit would be allowed. In essence, the game would begin again, but new players would be invited in.

Notes

1. See Foreign Tax Credits Claimed By U.S. Petroleum Companies; House of Representatives, Government Operations Committee; testimony of Mr. Jerome Kurz, Commissioner, Internal Revenue Service (November, 1977), p. 374.

2. U.S. Senate, Foreign Relations Committee, Subcommittee Report on Multinational Corporations, Washington, D.C., January 1975.

3. U.S. Senate Foreign Relations Committee, Multinational Subcommittee Report.

An Oil Futures Market

The development of an organized exchange market for oil products would help make the pricing process more competitive. Future contracts for certain oil products are now available for trading on the New York Mercantile Exchange. This open, visible pricing system for oil products would eliminate some of the need for excessive domestic regulation and thereby help both the Department of Energy (DOE) and the oil companies. To the extent that a surplus appears in the market, the trading of the futures contracts will help to insure that oil prices react. If product prices decline because of slow volume, this will be felt by the refiners who will ultimately cut their production, which in turn will feed back to the crude-oil suppliers. This process could then translate into lower crude-oil prices, as crude-oil suppliers compete for market share.

Dilution of OPEC's monopoly–price–setting capabilities would be further advanced by putting into place new mechanisms that limit the cartel's capability to dictate world oil prices unilaterally. One such mechanism would be the adoption of a market exchange system for international oil, regulated by representatives of both consuming and producing nations. With the consuming nations now able to exercise substantial market influence as a result of an increasing abundance of oil, I believe that this approach could be successfully applied.

In the international diplomatic arena, the U.S. government should move away from a Mercantilist conception of oil pricing and should urge that a market exchange system would be established to determine the price of oil, rather than accept the idea of an international treaty based on political perceptions of a fair price. No one ever really knows what a fair price is. Sellers believe that higher prices are fairer than lower prices. Buyers, on the other hand, think that lower prices are fairer than higher prices. Markets avoid the necessity for governments to decide what is a fair price. Appropriately regulated exchange markets offer the best mechanism for letting all buyers and sellers vote on what they think is a fair price.

The replacement cost of synthetic energy sources is not a realistic basis for oil pricing, because it implies that price is solely determined by supply, with little or no demand influences. Since oil is an internationally traded commodity, its price can be strongly influenced by demand factors, provided that the responding supply system is competitive. Neither is the index-ing of oil prices to world inflation a useful departure point for international negotiations. General economic inflation hurts both oil-consuming and oil-producing countries. If the price of a barrel of oil keeps rising to offset a loss of purchasing power in the oil-exporting countries, this compounds inflationary pressures in the oil-importing countries, causing the price of the world's non-oil goods and services to rise even further. Playing the game of catching up with inflation simply adds to the inflationary spiral. Ultimately someone loses out, and it is usually those with the least market leverage. An appropriately regulated market exchange system, however, would permit no one group of buyers or sellers to employ excessive market leverage. Prices go up when there are more buyers than sellers, and prices go down when there are more sellers than buyers. Unfortunately, this simple principle does not now apply in the monopolistic and political atmosphere of today's international oil markets. U.S. government policy should work toward stimulating a greater use of the free market mechanism in interna-tional oil and not simply acquiesce to present supply arrangements at monopolistic prices. No matter how orderly these market agreements may seem, they represent the cutting edge of monopoly control, the fixing by government fiat what is inherently a fluctuating process. The very stability that the orderly market agreement hopes to achieve is eventually under-mined by new competitive pressure and in the long run becomes detrimental to international political stability.

The Economic Role of Future Markets

I believe that a more positive approach to international oil problems would be to strengthen the marketplace through the use of organized exchanges, especially through the use of futures contracts. The economic function of futures markets is the transference of risk in highly competitive situations. Futures markets give buyers and sellers who do not want the risk of carrying inventories the opportunity to pass the risk on to those who do want it and the gains it might entail—the speculators. When production is carried on for a world market through a vast industrialized complex, there is an extended period of time between initial production and final use. There is also the risk that prices may move adversely at any time during the long period of production, storage, processing, distribution, and final use. Incurring this risk is a normal part of doing business; the futures market is one mechanism by which exposure to this particular business risk can be eliminated. The futures market offers an immediate elimination of price risk to the holder of inventory. By selling a futures contract at a fixed price, the holder of inventory is insulated from future market movements. In addition, in a period of rising inflation the commodity user can build up low-cost inventory by purchasing a futures contract. He can protect the profits from his futures sales against the possibility of higher prices for raw materials. The futures market can also be used to offset currency fluctuations and to increase the turnover of capital through loans on hedged commodities.

All organized exchange markets contain both a cash price for current transactions and a forward price reflecting the market's expectations of future price pressures. Economists have long regarded commodity markets as embodying many of the features of a truly competitive marketplace, where prices are always tending toward their equilibrium levels according to the laws of supply and demand. Indeed, futures markets are the closest real-world approximation to the ideal model of "perfect competition", which underlies many of the benefits of a free enterprise system. In a perfectly competitive market no single producer or consumer can affect the price of the product. Price formation is efficient, in the sense that knowledge of market developments is immediately transmitted to the central marketplace and is available to all market participants.

Commodity trading is often subjected to the criticism that the futures markets themselves increase price volatility and that speculators cause wild price swings that are unwarranted by underlying economic conditions. In recent years commodity futures trading has grown very rapidly; in 1977 an estimated trillion dollars worth of commodity contracts were traded in the United States, up from less than $200 billion just five years before. With that spectacular growth have come charges of scandal, real and imagined, often levied by those who have been hurt by adverse price movements. As a result, a number of politicians have claimed that commodity markets offer greater opportunities for price manipulation. Executives of some large corporations, whose pricing patterns are heavily influenced by commodity markets in the products that they sell, have often been critical of the unstable nature of the market system. Consumer groups have complained that particular agricultural commodity markets have contributed to inflationary pressures on food prices. Finally, on the international level, many less developed countries have been demanding buffer stock arrangements and other schemes to stabilize their earnings from raw material exports.

Typically, much of this criticism is misdirected and stems either from a lack of understanding or from an attempt to advance the critic's own position. Commodity markets are vulnerable to public criticism because they are highly visible to the public and the pricing process is open to all who care to examine it. Some excesses occur from time to time, but most can be attributed to poor regulatory procedures. The criticism of the corporate executive, however, derives from his desire to better control his own prices and from his own reluctance to use the exchange market for commercial hedging. To the consumer and to the politician, the pressure of rising prices, not the volatility per se is what counts. To the government of the less developed country, the pressure comes from the opposite side, namely, the effect of falling commodity prices, rather than the price fluctuation itself. But that is what free markets are all about, and the fact that organized exchanges provide a central marketplace for buyers and sellers to execute transactions is no reason to damn the process. I would claim that open, organized commodity exchanges substantially reduce the opportunity for price manipulation by any one party, simply because it is more difficult to employ excessive market leverage in an open and often sophisticated forum. In effect, the financial penalties for trying to manipulate a futures market can be quite severe, if the attempt is made to counter underlying economic pressures. Every futures contract has an expiration date, at which point its value equals the actual price in the cash market, as determined by supply and demand at the time of physical transactions. Any speculator who accumulates a long position in a commodity, adding to the upward pressure on prices, knows that he must eventually liquidate that position and thereby add to the downward pressure on prices. He can make a profit only if he forecasts correctly the overall trend of cash prices as determined by underlying economic conditions. The very size of most futures markets also argues against price manipulation, because these markets reflect the bids and offers of thousands of participants and deal with commodities that are produced and consumed on an international scale.

It is not the increased use of futures markets that causes price instability; increased instability has encouraged a greater use of futures markets. That instability has derived from changes in underlying economic and political trends, such as government dismantling of farm support programs, the new roles of China and Russia as large and unpredictable buyers in world agricultural markets, and a wave of heightened government intervention in worldwide markets, ranging from the sudden imposition of mining severance fees, export taxes, currency realignments, and export controls. Given the degree of disruption since 1973, one could even make the case that recent commodity price fluctuations have been relatively modest.

Over the years there have been numerous studies demonstrating the efficiency of commodities futures markets. If market information is instantly reflected in the price, movements in either direction will occur in a random fashion. Using this random–walk hypothesis as a test of market efficiency, these studies have overwhelmingly demonstrated that price fluctuations generated on organized commodity exchanges come as close to the perfectly competitive theoretical concept of pricing as is likely to occur in the real world. Such findings further show that speculation actually stabilizes prices by helping digest and transmit information rapidly. The greater the speculation in relation to purely commercial hedging, the smaller the spread between futures and spot prices. The market liquidity provided by speculation tends to reduce price distortions. In fact, some studies suggest that speculation helps contain excessive price movements. The futures pricing mechanism further contributes to price stability by providing information to the trade; even if businessmen do not take positions in the market themselves, the information itself helps them make more efficient inventory, production, and consumption decisions.

Barriers to Crude–Oil Futures Trading

In principle, an organized exchange market for crude oil operating on an international scale would be, in my judgment, the best approach to oil pricing. Properly regulated, to avoid both monopolistic and monopsonistic practices, such a market would reflect the true value of a barrel of oil at any point in time. That such commodity markets operate effectively in certain agricultural and metal products but do not exist for oil reflects historical, organizational, and technological differences. To overcome these differences in a short period of time or to force a crude–oil exchange market by government fiat would probably not be useful in the long run. Operational risks must be so great in existing distribution channels that private market participants will on their own initiative use a futures market.

Historically, crude–oil markets were largely controlled by refining interests; that is, prices were primarily dictated by the buyers of oil who had the ability to turn crude petroleum into useful products. Market dominance stemmed from the ability to satisfy a growing number of uses for petroleum products, with the coming of the automobile age, the electrificaton of the industrial economies, and more recently the growth of air travel, and the petrochemicals industry. As far back as the turn of the century the dominance of the Standard Oil Trust was largely a reflection of the drive by the refining and marketing segments of the oil business to obtain secure sources of raw material. In the United States the historical control of pipelines from the oilfields gave the crude–oil buyer the physical ability to dictate prices. Overseas it was the refining interests themselves who either discovered the crude–oil reserves or quickly bought out the independent concessionaire who might have discovered a major pool of oil. As a result, both vertical integration and the provision of an assured market for the growing volume of crude oil did not provide the incentive for the industry to develop a futures market. Large pools of oil were discovered from time to time, but these remained primarily in the hands of those who had their own refining and marketing outlets. In the United States where there were (and still are) a substantial number of independent oil companies on both sides of the crude–oil market, futures pricing never developed because the vertically integrated major oil companies provided both a stable outlet for the crude-oil seller and a stable supply source for the independent refiner. After discovery of oil in eastern Texas in the early 1930s, the market became so glutted that the state of Texas imposed a system of market demand prorationing which limited production of crude oil to those volumes that the major refining companies wished to purchase. In this way, the U.S. crude-oil market became effectively insulated from significant price pressures in the product market. The same type of market stability was achieved overseas through agreements among major oil companies to divide up the international markets. These agreements were often sanctioned by the European governments which did not have the same opposition to cartels as did the United States.

There were other reasons why a crude-oil futures market never developed. First, there were not enough independent participants. Second, the time required from production of crude oil from known reservoirs to the consumption of the crude oil in the refinery was not long enough to impose unacceptable risks on buyer and seller. In copper production and in agriculture the uncertainty imposed by long lead times is one of the important reasons why futures markets have developed. The long lead times in the oil business occur in the exploration and development phase, prior to the installation of producing capacity.

Nevertheless, since a greater degree of control of the crude-oil market has now shifted to the producing countries, there may be a case for the development of an international crude-oil futures market. Technical problems abound, however, such as quality differentials among crude oils which cannot be easily transferred from one refinery to another. Sufficient storage capacity at particular distribution centers is another problem. Most important, under OPEC pricing practices, which are at least tacitly condoned by both certain international oil companies and by certain oil-consuming governments, there is not enough price fluctuation to justify a full-fledged futures market at the present time. I believe, however, that the OPEC takeover of the pricing mechanism, coupled with producer-country ownership of the crude oil itself, will gradually require new market mechanisms with a much greater degree of arm's-length bargaining between crude-oil seller and purchasing refiner. This is indicated by the sharp increase in crude-oil trading since 1974, although the major part of this trading still represents a rearrangement of distribution patterns more than a shopping for better prices. As time goes on, however, more independent crude-oil sources will develop, and the buyers' leverage will return. As this occurs over the next several years, both buying and selling interests in the crude-oil market may well turn to an organized exchange mechanism for pricing.

Petroleum Products: An Initial Step

As a step toward the return of more competitive crude-oil pricing, I believe that a futures market in petroleum products could work today. Appropriately structured and regulated, it should be in the interest of most market participants, including refiners, various types of distribution firms, and large final users. Figure 8-1 illustrates the current distribution channels and the interface with a futures market. Three conditions are necessary for a futures market to function as a complementary pricing system to the cash market. First, there must be a large number of buyers and sellers, so that a substantial and continuous flow of bids and offers will be maintained. Second, there must be enough price fluctuation in the cash market to provide the incentive to reduce financial risk through the purchase of futures contracts. Price volatility often relates to fluctuations in volume, usually resulting from both seasonal and cyclical market pressures. Wholesale markets in petroleum products satisfy both these criteria. The third condition that is necessary for effective futures trading is adequate storage capacity. This could be a problem in certain parts of the country where a

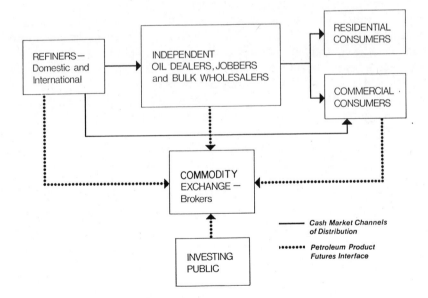

Figure 8-1. Interrelationship of Petroleum Product Futures and Cash Market Channels of Distribution

petroleum product futures market might develop. Some commodity exchanges maintain minimum storage capacity, which is jointly owned by exchange members, such as with copper traded on the London Metal Exchange. Other exchanges rely primarily on the storage capacity of the industry, which may be far-flung geographically so that delivery on a futures contract must be adjusted to account for transport costs from warehouse to market. This applies to a number of agricultural commodities traded in the Chicago futures markets. In all cases, however, the futures markets work because industry participants prefer to hedge the price risks associated with carrying inventory, and there are speculators in the market who are willing to assume those risks.

In the case of a petroleum product futures market, one serious technical barrier appears to be inadequate storage to make the delivery system credible to potential users. While in reality this delivery and storage issue may not be a barrier, the perception of potential difficulties with exchange delivery patterns, may impede the open-market trading of a petroleum futures contract. If the case can be made that it would be in the public interest to have a futures market in petroleum products, then the federal government could undertake to build such storage capacity. This storage could become part of the Strategic Petroleum Reserve, the funds for which have already been authorized by the Congress. Although the federal government would own the warehouse, the oil in the warehouse could be owned by private market participants. A person who sold a "short" contract in the futures market, who contracted to deliver oil at some point in the future, could use this warehouse to make his delivery. On the other hand, he might choose not to deliver in which case he might buy back his short contract, or he might choose to deliver in another manner specified in the terms of the futures contract. At the same time, someone who purchased a "long" contract in the futures market, who contracted to buy oil at some point in the future, could use this warehouse to take his delivery. Again, the holder of the long contract could either sell out the contract prior to delivery date or accept delivery in another prespecified manner. In other words, use of the government warehouse would not be mandatory, but it would add a substantial degree of credibility to the futures market mechanism. This approach has been successfully applied by the government to many agricultural storage programs over the years.

Potential Participants

Changes in the worldwide oil industry since 1974 suggest that current petroleum product market participants would stand to gain from the use of a futures market. The principal group likely to find a futures market advantageous are the resellers, those who buy from a refiner and redistribute either to other distributors or to final users. This group includes jobbers, terminal operators, gasoline wholesalers, heating oil dealers, and oil trading firms. There are thousands of these firms in the United States, with the heaviest concentration in the Northeast and Midwest. They would be ideally situated to take advantage of a petroleum product futures market.

A number of current economic pressures suggest that this market could quickly become viable. First, these reseller groups face soaring inventory costs, several times higher than they were just a few years ago. At the same time, however, growth in volume has slowed as oil users have moved to conserve the higher-cost fuel. As a result, profit margins have been squeezed, despite higher product prices. In this environment a reseller could at least partially hedge his inventory position by using futures contracts. The reseller can accomplish this by buying a long contract today, thereby fixing his costs, and at the same time selling a short contract, thereby fixing his revenues. His profit margin is thus protected from future swings in the market prices that he receives and in the costs that he incurs. A second factor likely to stimulate reseller interest relates to the increasing reluctance of major oil companies to absorb normal volume fluctuations which the reseller typically experiences. In the past the major oil company supplier would take back excess oil from the reseller if he had purchased too much or supply the reseller with more oil if he had ordered too little. This was done without substantial financial penalty to the reseller, because the major company was big enough to absorb these normal operating contingencies. The major company was more than compensated for any financial loss through profits on its crude oil. Today industry economics for the major companies have put pressure on crude-oil profits, and the major oil companies do not have the financial cushion to be the shock absorbers to the independent reseller distribution business. Crude-oil profits have shrunk because of the rising OPEC "take" internationally and the heavy regulations domestically. Since the major oil companies, therefore, must try to improve their refining margins through higher revenues, they can no longer afford to absorb the business risks of the reseller. Over the past few years an increasing number of major oil companies have been moving toward greater length relationships with their reseller companies, repurchasing or resupplying oil at market prices, and thus requiring the distributors to better plan their own operations. A futures market could be a valuable tool to these resellers in this new environment.

Other potential users of the futures market in petroleum products include refiners (major company and independent), electric utilities, chemical firms, shipping firms, and other large industrial and commercial users of petroleum products. In addition, some foreign national oil companies may find it advantageous to hedge their crude-oil and product sales through the use of futures contracts. In fact, natural arbitrage would likely develop between spot crude-oil prices and future product prices, so that sellers of crude oil could also become active in the product futures market.

The Market as Marginal Cost Mechanism

In the United States today gasoline, distillate, and residual fuel are consumed at the rate of around 14 million barrels per day (MMB/D), accounting for almost three-fourths of U.S. oil consumption. If a futures market were to obtain 5 percent of that volume, or 700,000 barrels per day, then it would likely set the pricing patterns for the remaining 95 percent of the transactions. Market prices reflect incremental, or marginal, purchases and sales where existing buyers and sellers are either long or short relative to their anticipated positions. Futures markets reflect a consensus view of these expectations, and transaction prices in existing markets cannot deviate substantially from spot prices as determined in a commodity exchange market. Visible alternatives always exist to both buyer and seller when a commodity is traded in an open exchange system. Although most transactions will not be done by the commodity exchange, the prices at which these transactions occur will be done at levels dictated by the exchange. If either buyer or seller tries to move too far from the exchange-determined price, the other party has the alternative of transacting his business through the exchange.

The copper industry has important analogies to the petroleum business. There are large, integrated companies operating on a worldwide scale. A majority of transactions are done directly by buyers and sellers, many of whom are very large firms. There is even an OPEC-like organization, called CIPEC (Council of Copper Exporting Countries), based in Paris and composed of Zaire, Zambia, Peru, and Chile. That CIPEC has not attained OPEC's success is partly because of the existence of the London Metal Exchange and its younger American counterpart, the Comex in New York. The price of copper is determined on these exchanges by an open auction technique. Most physical market participants maintain relationships with exchange brokers who execute their orders. These orders from the copper trade itself represent the effects of unanticipated events, for example, when a seller has more physical supplies than he can sell directly to his customers or when a copper user has not ordered enough from his traditional supplier. In the copper futures market the flow of orders represents both commercial hedging and speculation. The volumes of copper that move through exchanges, where physical delivery actually occurs, represent no more than 5 percent of the worldwide transactions in copper. Yet the entire copper industry, buyer and seller alike, must use the prices set by these commodity exchanges. Nobody particularly likes it, but they must all obey the discipline of the market.

Public Policy Implications

I believe that a futures market in petroleum products would have the following beneficial effects:

1. Petroleum product prices can have an important impact on crude-oil prices, provided that there is a mechanism for insuring that buyers have as much leverage in the market as sellers. A petroleum product futures market would permit buyers to use that leverage more effectively. During periods of surplus markets, declines in product prices would back into crude-oil markets more rapidly than under the present system. That is, as buyers of petroleum products throughout the distribution chain bid down product prices, the refiner would have to either cut back his refinery runs until the product surplus disappears or seek lower crude-oil prices from his suppliers. The refiner will take both of these actions to varying degrees today, but with the advent of futures trading, a declining product futures price would give an important early warning signal to crude-oil suppliers. These crude-oil producers, private oil companies, and OPEC national oil companies alike would then react by either reducing crude-oil production or decreasing crude-oil prices. Each seller would have to react faster and to a greater degree than under the present system, thereby generating the potential for more competition among crude-oil suppliers. Since the history of the petroleum industry has been one of surplus, and in my judgment that surplus is likely to continue, the futures market could represent a limited but still important mechanism by which that surplus can be more visibly and rapidly translated into lower product prices.

2. Critics of the petroleum industry have argued that vertical divestiture would be an important step in making the industry more competitive. (That is, breaking up the oil companies into their functional parts, crude-oil exploration and production, transport, refining, and marketing.) Presumably this greater degree of competition would lead to lower product prices for the consumer. The development of a futures market for petroleum products would accomplish at least part of the goal of vertical divestiture, primarily as it affects relationships between refineries and their product distribution channels. Transfer prices for petroleum products based primarily on crude-oil costs would be modified to reflect demand conditions in the market, as greater arm's-length negotiation of product prices became reflected on the exchange market. Yet this goal would be achieved without having to upset current patterns of ownership and distribution.

3. An open and visible pricing mechanism would reduce the allegation

by oil industry critics that current product pricing practices are not competitive. It should be in the interest of the major oil companies to encourage this open-market pricing concept, thereby relieving some of their heavy regulatory burdens and refuting the substantial misunderstandings that have occurred between the public and the oil industry. This could also reduce some of the regulatory burden on the federal government and thus reduce the size of the now burgeoning energy regulatory bureaucracy. Commodity exchange pricing, reflecting true supply and demand conditions in an open, central marketplace, should be preferable to filling out voluminous forms on the part of industry and to creating and analyzing those forms on the part of government. More paperwork is not likely to lead to a better pricing mechanism.

The reaction of the major oil companies to this proposal is likely to be one of considerable skepticism. This response should be understood in the context of traditional industry practices, which are for the most part highly competitive in U.S. product markets. The only rational objection to the growth of a futures market on the part of the companies is that their pricing control will be at least partially diluted. It is doubtful that they would state this publicly, and a smokescreen of other objections is likely to emerge. My own response is that since the control of crude-oil pricing has at least in part shifted to OPEC, the ultimate consumers of petroleum products should be given a chance to better respond in the marketplace. This will put an added burden on the oil companies in controlling their refining margins but may also be helpful to them in bargaining with OPEC crude-oil suppliers. The oil industry is being forced reluctantly into trying new approaches and the futures market could be a valuable addition to this process of industry change.

The reaction of the U.S. government to this proposal is also likely to be one of skepticism. The notion that futures markets are gambling casinos is a misconception held by many in government. More important, the advent of a successful futures market could eventually eliminate the need for product price controls, product allocations, and even entitlements. To the extent that this threatens the position of the regulator, it is not likely to be warmly received in certain Washington quarters. Nevertheless, with the benefits to the public that could emerge from such a market, this opposition can probably be overcome.

9

Financing Oil Exploration

The U.S. government, together with other international financial agencies, should aid in the financing of oil exploration outside the United States, primarily in the non–OPEC developing countries. The benefits of this policy should be apparent in terms of potentially adding to the world's supplies of oil and gas, in terms of relieving the balance–of–payments position of some of these countries, in terms of diluting some of OPEC's price–setting powers, and finally in terms of encouraging more competition in international oil markets. This additional financing should be complementary to the private sector, engaging in those ventures where the economic or political risks may be too great for private industry.

The first three recommendations in this book, dealing with import quotas, foreign tax credits, and petroleum product pricing, pertain to changing the terms under which existing oil is imported and priced. In this chapter the subject is how to increase worldwide supplies of new oil, especially in non–OPEC developing countries. If new oil reserves were discovered in these areas, the benefits to the world economy could be substantial, in terms of reducing the balance–of–payments pressure on these nations, increasing competition among oil suppliers, and restraining further price rises by OPEC. To accomplish this goal, if it can be done at all, enormous sums of capital are required. Since the international oil companies and the OPEC countries are reluctant to invest heavily in potential new sources of supply, it will be up to the governments of the industrial, oil–consuming nations to finance such a program.

What could such a financing program achieve? How big should it be? What role should the financing agency play in the negotiations between the oil operator and the host government? The answers to these and other related questions are important to the success of any government oil–related venture–capital investment.

It is an obvious, and sometimes overlooked, fact that prior to the development of known oil structures, massive sums for exploration must be spent. In frontier area wildcatting nine out of ten wells are usually dry. But unless these nine dry holes are drilled, with the resulting funds literally poured down a hole, the tenth producing well will not be found. The game of wildcat oil exploration is not normally played very well by bureaucrats, in governments or in giant corporations. To drill that tenth successful well, the driller must have optimism, nerve, freedom of action, and a shrewd gambling instinct, traits not commonly associated with most government or corporate executives.

It will take financial incentives to encourage the oil wildcatter into the non–OPEC developing countries. The geological risks are high, but the political risks can be even higher. If oil (or natural gas) is in fact discovered, what is to prevent the host government from changing the terms of its initial prediscovery agreement with the wildcatter? These and related problems can best be handled by the governments of the United States and other industrial, oil-consuming nations, because of the leverage that they can exercise on the host government should it renege on its initial commitments.

Current Barriers to Exploration in the Developing Countries

There are at least four types of impediments to increased oil exploration in the developing countries. First, present concession or purchasing arrangements between OPEC member governments and international oil companies might be endangered if some of these companies were to embark on major new exploration efforts. This is amply demonstrated by the testimony of a former Exxon executive before the hearings of the Senate Subcommittee on Multinational Corporations. When asked by Senator Charles Percy of Illinois why Exxon turned down an opportunity to develop a 10 billion barrel field in Oman, the Exxon executive specifically replied that he thought it would endanger the Aramco concession because any new oil from Oman would compete with existing oil from Saudi Arabia, thereby angering the Saudi government should Exxon have to reduce its production of Saudi oil to make way for new oil production in Oman.

> I'm sure there is a 10 billion barrel field there, and I'm absolutely sure we don't want to go into it. I might put some money into it if I was sure we weren't going to get some oil, but not if we are going to get oil because we are liable to lose the Aramco concession.[1]

There was nothing insidious about this remark, as long as the international oil market was competitive. With OPEC dictating the terms today, however, some international oil companies have lost their leverage, or at least have chosen not to exercise it.

The second barrier to increased exploration in the non–oil developing countries by the major international companies is the oil surplus itself. No private firm steps up its investment in new capacity if it projects surplus markets ahead. This is essentially true in oil exploration, where the randomness of the discovery process can quickly upset the most thorough projections. If the international oil companies in fact foresee a significant tightening of world markets by 1985, then they would be investing much larger sums in worldwide oil exploration, despite the geological and political risks. But, as captives of OPEC, their incentives today are to cooperate with the contrived scarcity of the cartel.

A third barrier relates to the provision of a market for oil that might be exported from a developing country. Depending on the type of crude oil and where it is located in the world, provision of transportation to refining centers is not always automatic. While this is not a major constraint, it is an additional cost that must be accounted for in calculating the competitiveness of a potential new oil field.

The last and most serious limitation involves the availability of capital to those smaller companies who have little or no connection with OPEC production and have traditionally been reluctant to venture overseas in any major way. This reluctance stems from a combination of geological and political risk relative to the amounts of capital that these independent companies can invest. For example, $200 million of equity investment, the majority of which would be spent in wildcat exploration, is needed to discover a 1 billion barrel field and to achieve a rate of return commensurate with the risk and the probable host government's proportion of 75 to 95 percent. If a $200 million equity investment establishes the dimensions of the petroleum reservoirs, it could take another $800 million to develop the field. Typically, this money could be borrowed, but interest costs are high and bankers are not always willing to assume the risks. The debt capital would be used for development wells which could establish a production rate of around 200,000 barrels per day or 70 million barrels per year. If the company can retain $0.50 per barrel after it pays its U.S. taxes, the company could then earn a competitive return of 15 percent to 20 percent on its equity capital. The statistical potential for finding fields of a billion barrels or more is small. Only some 120 oil fields with 1 or more billion barrels have been discovered worldwide since the birth of the oil industry over one hundred years ago. While geological prospects are promising in many parts of the world, unstable host governments and competitive low-cost Mideastern oil as a potential market threat make the purely private enterprise risks very high.

Geological Potential

According to many geologists, the oil potential of the developing countries is excellent. Bernado F. Grossling, the senior research geophysicist for the

U.S. Geological Survey, estimates that as much as one-half of all the world's undiscovered petroleum could be in the developing countries. Table 9-1 shows where the oil might be found and how it compares to existing proven reserves today.

As table 9-1 shows, the non-Communist world outside OPEC has only about 100 billion barrels of proven reserves, while OPEC has close to 500 billion barrels. The developing countries, however, could eventually add as much oil to the world's reserves as OPEC has today, according to Grossling's low estimate. According to the high estimate, these developing nations could almost quadruple those reserves.

The outstanding example of this potential is Mexico, whose proven reserves at the end of 1976 stood at about 7 billion barrels, 5 billion of which were discovered in 1975 and 1976. By the end of 1978 Mexican proven reserves had risen to 30 billion barrels; probable Mexican reserves are estimated at over 60 billion barrels, with additional potential reserves of another 100 billion to 200 billion barrels. In other words, the geological

Table 9-1
Estimated Oil Potential of the Non-OPEC Developing Countries, January 1, 1978
(billions of barrels)

Region	Low Estimate	High Estimate
Latin America	215	790
Africa (including Madagascar)	160	625
South and Southeast Asia	90	300
China	27	172
Total	492	1,887
Proven Reserves		
Non-OPEC		
United States and Canada	37	
Latin America	20	
Africa	5	
Asia	6	
Western Europe	30	
Communist countries	100	
Total	198	
OPEC		
Mideast	390	
Africa	55	
Latin America	20	
Asia	15	
Total	480	

Sources: *Business Week,* July 10, 1978, p. 64. Cited from Bernado F. Grossling, U.S. Geological Survey. Proven reserves data from American Petroleum Institute.

potential that had existed prior to 1974 had never been exploited. When OPEC quadrupled world oil prices in 1974, the Mexican government decided to invest the vast sums needed to turn geologic potential into the actual capacity to produce oil. If it worked in Mexico, it could work in other parts of the world.

According to A.A. Meyerhoff, a prominent consulting geologist writing in the Seventy-Fifth Anniversary issue of the *Oil and Gas Journal* (August 1977), there are some fifty-five promising new onshore areas around the world, outside the Communist nations. Of these, twenty-five lie in developed Western nations or in OPEC countries. Of the remaining thirty areas, fifteen are in Central and South America and the Caribbean, five in Africa, and ten in the developing nations of Asia. Although Meyerhoff gives no potential reserve figures, his survey suggests that the geologic potential is excellent. Offshore, where the giant oil fields have been found, the geologic potential is even greater. According to H.D. Klemme, writing in the same issue of the *Oil and Gas Journal,* some sixty giant offshore fields have been found in the past, either partially or totally offshore. These are located either in inland seas or in continental shelf areas. Half of these represent the early discovery and development phase of offshore activity and are located partially offshore and partially onshore. The other half are totally offshore and represent developments since the late 1950s. The totally offshore fields appear to be on average of smaller size than those partially onshore. Klemme concludes that the better potential, therefore, lies in these partially onshore-offshore areas, many of which lie in the world's outer continental shelves. He identifies about sixty potential areas, half in the non-Communist, non-OPEC developing nations. These include areas off the coasts of Brazil and Argentina, much of the huge coast of West Africa, Madagascar, India and Bangladesh, and Southeast Asia. He estimates that as much as 40 percent of the world's remaining discoverable reserves could be found in these giant fields—between 1 and 2 trillion barrels of oil.

The potential thus appears excellent, but the time required to explore and develop any one of these frontier areas could be in the range of seven to twelve years. Nonetheless, these lead times are not particularly long, relative to the lead times involved in producing synthetic oil or gas from shale or coal. They are much shorter than the estimated time needed to make solar energy economic. In fact, in terms of timing, development of conventional oil and gas reserves in promising geologic areas around the world represents the most rapid answer to any possible tightening of world oil markets in the late 1980s or early 1990s. While any oil discovered in these non-OPEC developing countries would not be under U.S. control, the greater diversity of supply sources would add importantly to U.S. buying leverage in world oil markets. After all, once the oil is discovered, these nations will want to sell it. The more of it there is to be sold, the less the upward pressures on oil prices.

Role of Government

U.S. government financing of oil exploration in non–OPEC developing countries would represent a practical and positive step toward the alleviation of many of the world's energy-related problems. If other oil-consuming countries can be brought in, the exploration fund could be expanded that much more. The efforts of the World Bank in this regard deserve considerable encouragement, but other international pressures are not likely to make that institution a major source of financing for exploration.

To date the U.S. government (the Carter administration) has been very slow to respond to proposals in this area. In the departments of State, Treasury, and Energy some ideas on funding oil development, rather than exploration, in non–OPEC developing countries have been lingering for some time. For the most part, however, these proposals focus on providing assistance after oil (or gas) has been discovered, under the rationale that U.S. government funds and influence can best be used to reduce political risk that occurs only after oil is discovered. That is, if the private oil operator drills only dry holes, there are no spoils to argue over. Only after oil has been discovered would there by any incentive for a host government to change the terms of the initial agreement. U.S. government loans for the development of the already discovered oil might be used to restrain the appetite of the host government. But the exploratory risk, both financial and geological, would still be borne by the private oil company.

This approach, favored by certain Carter administration officials, is not likely to produce a single barrel of oil that would not be had otherwise, although the development process might be speeded up somewhat. The reason is that once oil is found in an exploratory area, private sector development funds can usually be obtained. "Development money is bankable" is the oil industry phrase for describing that banks will loan money to oil operators to drill wells in areas where exploration has already established the existence of oil in large enough quantities to justify development of the field. U.S. government diplomatic influence can be helpful in preventing a host government from trying to rewrite the terms of an initial contract, but this is usually available in any case and does not increase the incentive for private operators to explore for oil in frontier areas outside of the United States. A somewhat more positive approach has been taken by the U.S. government's Overseas Private Investment Corporation (OPIC) in insuring the private oil operator from expropriation or other damages that he might suffer from a host government's action against him. Again, however, neither the geologic nor financial risks are reduced by this insurance program.

A federally financed program of wildcat exploration in non–OPEC developing countries is required. Government funds would complement private sector capital, and the government would be entitled to its share of those benefits that normally accrue to those who bear the front-end risk. The Japanese, for example, have financed oil exploration in many parts of the world through a wholly owned government corporation, the Japanese Petroleum Development Company. This company operates worldwide and is largely a financial entity whose role is to enter joint ventures with operating oil companies. The Japanese provide a portion of the exploratory funds, will help in securing development loans should oil be discovered, and in some cases exercise a certain influence over royalty and tax terms with host governments. In return, the Japanese get first call on any oil that may be produced, as well as the usual financial returns. Many other industrial countries maintain actual operating oil companies that engage in the search for oil on a worldwide basis. Only the U.S. government has virtually no effort in this area.

When the private sector in the United States cannot or will not perform a function that is clearly in the public interest, then it is an accepted practice for government to see that the job gets done. When the Soviet Union fired the Sputnik rocket into space in 1956, the U.S. government quickly reacted to what was perceived as a potential threat to American national security. Although further U.S. government involvement in the private sector can often create more problems than it solves, the political and economic dimensions of our present oil problems are so far-reaching that some government involvement has become necessary. The trouble is that government has never focused on the true nature of the crisis—OPEC control of world oil supplies and prices. Although government should not be encouraged to interfere in the free market system, as it is in the domestic oil business, a stronger government role in the international oil business should be developed, because the free market no longer operates internationally due to the market control exercised by the OPEC cartel. Federal government financing of foreign oil exploration would help bring about a more competitive market in the international oil trade by providing alternative sources to OPEC production.

The first principle of federal financing of oil exploration in the developing nations should be to enter the planning process at an early phase. An agency of government should be established to keep an inventory of new exploration possibilities, a flow of information on both geological and political developments in these areas, and a financing capability to enter into joint ventures with private sector capital sources that might have an interest in starting an oil exploration program. This agency should publicize its information and financing capabilities to the oil industry and to existing financial institutions, so that a flow of proposals into the agency will be established. A second principle should be to share the risk with private capital during the exploration phase. A flexible policy on the proportion financed by the government on any particular deal should be followed, but some operating guidelines on the total portfolio of exploration loans could be established. For example, a rule that the government share of the totality of its financing should not exceed 50 percent of the private sector capital might be a reasonable way to start. In addition, portfolio diversification in terms of geology, geography, and political risk would be important and businesslike operating criteria. A third principle should be to finance only independent oil operators, or at least those who have only limited involvement with OPEC oil sources. Some discretion in this regard would have to be given to the administrator of the proposed agency, but the clear intent of the enterprise should be to encourage a greater diversity of worldwide oil supplies than exists at present.

The initial capital of this government fund would have to be in the range of a billion dollars, if the effort is going to have any substantial effect on the direction of worldwide oil exploration. Worldwide exploration expenditures outside the United States and Canada, the Communist bloc, and the OPEC countries, are probably no more than $2 billion annually, so that if the proposed government agency were to expend $200 million per year over five years, it would amount to around 10 percent of existing expenditures in those areas. But this 10 percent could make a difference. If the 50 percent rule proposed were adhered to, then the billion dollars of government financing would be coupled with another billion dollars of private sector funds. Thus $400 million per year might be expended in this type of exploratory effort over a five-year period. This could involve as few as two to three new deals per year to as many as twenty, depending on sizes of the potential ventures. To the extent that $200 million invested in wildcat exploration might eventually identify 1 billion barrels of new oil reserves, the expenditure of $2 billion over a five-year period could ultimately yield 10 billion barrels of new oil reserves. Using a fifteen-year producing life, this could mean adding 2 million barrels per day of production to world supplies, or about 4 percent of the non-Communist world's current consumption.

These figures deliberately exclude development funds, which could run four to five times the exploration expenditures. Nevertheless, the estimated costs for conventional exploration and development are typically far lower than the costs of developing synthetic supplies (oil shale, tar sands, or coal-based oil or gas). Even in the smallest fields of the North Sea, probably the most expensive conventional oil to date, exploration and development costs never ran more than $6 to $7 per barrel, which is only 25 to 30 percent of the estimated costs of these synthetics. In the relatively more hospitable climates of the developing nations, per barrel costs would probably run far lower than those in the North Sea. Thus the broad proposition makes sense financially.

The policy also makes sense economically, if our goal is to limit future upward pressures on international oil prices. While $1 billion seems like a lot of money, the cost to the U.S. economy of a $1 per barrel increase in OPEC prices is a $3 billion loss of direct consumer purchasing power, plus at least that much more in indirect ripple effects. The costs to the world economy are three times as great as to the U.S. economy. Such federal government investment would yield the highest and most rapid return of any new supply proposal now being considered in the energy field.

Possible Criticisms

Politically, such a program of federal government financing of oil exploration in non–OPEC developing countries raises a number of serious criticisms. The first objection will come from the U.S. taxpayer who can legitimately ask whether his tax dollars are not better spent in the United States and by the private sector. However, the U.S. exploratory effort is at an all-time high (despite environmentally motivated delays). Financial incentives for new oil in the United States are the highest in the world, and the political risk to the oil operator is the lowest in the world. The problem is that the geological potential in the United States is probably not sufficient in itself to ultimately yield enough oil to challenge OPEC's dominance over world oil supplies. If the dilution of the cartel's price–setting powers is a worthy goal of national energy policy, then restriction of federal government energy investments to the United States alone only impedes the achievement of that goal. The United States has a substantial number of independent oil operators who have the technical knowledge and experience to find oil anywhere in the world. These men also have the risk–taking penchant that made the oil and gas industry the dominant energy source that it is today. They lack the capital to venture overseas in a major way. U.S. government financial and diplomatic assistance would be a powerful vehicle to unleash that capability.

Another objection to this proposal will come from those in private industry or academia who will argue that the federal bureaucracy would be incapable of operating such a financing agency. That criticism is not without merit, largely because federal conflict–of–interest rules are so rigid that experienced oil men and bankers could be barred from working for this agency. Nevertheless, a separate corporation could be established, analogous to the Communications Satellite Corporation (COMSAT), which could take responsibility for this program. Being less political than a specific branch of government, this new federal oil financing corporation could enlist the experienced people who would be needed. A substantial amount of private sector skills would have to be used in assessing particular ventures and thereby preventing needless growth in personnel and red tape. Although independent U.S. oil men are likely to express an initial negative reaction to this proposal, they would quickly jump on the bandwagon when they recognized the inherent financial advantages that such a program would offer them.

A final criticism of this proposal could come from the foreign policy establishment itself. They may argue that such a program would complicate our diplomatic relations with the developing countries where some of the money would be invested, with OPEC governments who might have a natural suspicion of our motives, and with our oil-consuming-country allies who might want to purchase oil. All these complications would arise only if substantial amounts of new oil were discovered. We should welcome these potential complications, because they would mean that other governments would be recognizing the increased leverage that the United States would have gained in international oil negotiations.

Notes

1. Testimony of Howard Page before the Senate Subcommittee on Multinational Corporations, 1975.

10 Political Constraints: Real and Imagined

None of these recommendations alone is likely to be sufficient to dilute OPEC's hold on world oil prices. Taken together, however, they would certainly alter the expectations of oil market participants, both private companies and governments. Nevertheless, for the U.S. government to adopt these approaches, some of the concern over offending certain OPEC members would have to be lessened. Oil remains as much a commercial question as a political one. OPEC is a seller; the United States is a buyer. Our market interests diverge. We can still be the best of political allies with the member governments of OPEC, but we can also bargain with them over the price of oil. I believe that the broad approach to international oil-pricing problems should be to take the politics out of it as much as possible.

Choices of alternative solutions to our energy problems are constrained by an immense array of conflicting political pressures. Some of these political perceptions derive from the prospect of real economic and social change. A number of other political attitudes, particularly with regard to foreign policy, however, seem to be more imagined than real. If the recommendations proposed in this book are to be seriously considered, it will be necessary to sort out these political constraints, to analyze their source, and to determine the degree of validity that each argument and counterargument contains. Although politics is the art of the possible, economic forces often underpin many conflicting political perceptions.

I have divided these issues into those relating to domestic economic policy and those relating to foreign policy, both economic and diplomatic. It is in the latter area, I believe, that the more fundamental political constraints lie, primarily because prevailing political attitudes are derived from long-standing intellectual and emotional commitments.

Economic Policy

In chapter 9 I proposed that the U.S. government establish a $1 billion fund to promote worldwide oil exploration. To keep that proposition fiscally sound I suggest that the revenues gained by the Treasury through the elimination of certain foreign tax credits, amounting to $1 billion to $2 billion annually, (chapter 7), be used to fund this exploration effort. This reduction of present oil-company revenues and its diversion through the federal government to promote international oil exploration will be severely criticized by many oilmen, especially by the executives of the international oil companies. They will argue that the income from the foreign tax credit, which is being reinvested in worldwide exploration, is vital to their cash flow. Why take away these revenues on the one hand and reinvest them in the oil business on the other, especially with another government agency to be created in the middle? My answer is simple. The companies who would be losing the tax credit would not, for the most part, be the same companies that would participate in the proposed oil-exploration fund. The motive behind this redistribution of oil-industry revenues is to further weaken the symbiotic relationship between some OPEC governments and some major American international companies. If an oil company with no links to OPEC discovers oil somewhere in the world, its incentive to develop and produce that oil is substantially greater than if the same pool of oil were discovered by a company with established links to OPEC. In other words, it would stimulate international competition.

The incentives for those major oil companies that are losing revenues as a result of the loss of foreign tax credits, however, would be directed toward greater domestic exploration as a result of my proposal to totally decontrol domestic oil prices. The U.S. government should impose an extra-profits tax coupled with an exploration plow-back credit. These same companies would quickly take advantage of that financial incentive and in all likelihood step up their exploration programs in the United States. With the import price differential in the hands of the government the direct cost to the U.S. consumer need not rise above what it would be under the present system. Indirectly, of course, the budget deficit created by maintaining the import subsidy would be borne by the American public, but the magnitude of it would likely decline as time went on. Either more domestic oil would be found at presumably higher costs, thereby raising the direct costs to the U.S. consumer, which could not be helped in any event; or foreign oil prices would be reduced because of increased international competition. The course that the United States steers between these two forces will certainly involve political pressures as time goes on but with the goal of minimizing oil imports at the lowest possible costs. The present system maximizes imports, and because of the market distortions caused by price controls and entitlements, the price-dampening effects of domestic competition are themselves diluted.

The declared energy-policy goal of the Carter administration is to promote ever-higher oil prices for the U.S. consumer. Although domestic oil companies would receive only a portion of those increased revenues under the principle of a fair sharing of the burden, any proposed crude-oil tax has no limit. At present the tax would raise U.S. prices from $10 to $15 per barrel, the latter including the delivery cost of foreign oil. But because such a program offers no counter to OPEC's control of world oil prices, what happens to the crude-oil tax if OPEC were to raise prices to $20 or even to $25 per barrel? Presumably the U.S. government would keep increasing the tax or else permit a new differential between foreign and domestic prices to rise again. There would be no stopping it, because many in the present energy bureaucracy favor ever-higher oil prices in the belief that they stimulate new supplies and encourage conservation. Both arguments are not only fallacious but are damaging to U.S. interests, both economically and politically.

With regard to price-induced conservation, the world is already adjusting painfully to the initial quintupling of international oil prices. Ever-higher prices would not speed up that adjustment process. Industrial conservation is already taking place to the extent that energy-efficient substitutes are available. When these substitutes are either unavailable or too costly, higher fuel costs are simply passed on to the consumer. Ever-higher oil prices, because of their drain on consumer purchasing power, deter the capital investment decision and thereby slow the trend toward industrial conservation. Much of the incentive to install new capital equipment comes from the decision to first expand capacity and then, only secondarily, to implement that expansion with more energy-efficient equipment. Unless the economy's momentum is maintained, the capacity-expanding investment decision will not be made. With the consumer spending proportionately more on fuel and less on other goods and services, overall consumer demand will not grow as rapidly as it would in the absence of even higher oil prices. In other words, it seems to me that the price is high enough already to induce industrial conservation, which is already going on at a pace consistent with the private sector's balancing of higher energy costs with consumer demand growth.

On the other hand, direct fuel consumption by individuals is much more price inelastic than fuel demand by business. To suggest that even greater conservation by individuals would occur as a result of even higher prices flies in the face of both logic and econometric studies of retail oil markets. The proper approach, in my judgment, is to require consumer-goods manufacturers to make more fuel-efficient cars, oil burners, and household appliances. This process is already taking place and will be strengthened somewhat by some of the sections of the energy bill recently passed by the Congress.

It is undoubtedly true that higher domestic oil prices will induce more domestic conventional oil supplies. How high that price should go depends on how much self-sufficiency we, as a body politic, deem necessary for our political and economic independence. Prices for newly discovered domestic oil are likely to increase as geology and economics dictate higher U.S. finding costs. The U.S. market will tell us those numbers gradually and accurately, if the domestic market is insulated from OPEC's monopoly pricing by the imposition of a quota and if it is permitted to operate competitively without excessive interference from Washington. On the other hand, international oil prices are certainly high enough today to stimulate worldwide exploration, and the barriers to a more rapid expansion of that effort have little relationship to present price incentives. These impediments involve political risk in unstable host countries, a lack of capital by those who would accelerate the drilling, and a lack of incentive or fear of reprisal by those who have the capital but are content with their present international reserve positions. Finally, higher international oil prices are not likely to bring on synthetic energy supplies any more rapidly than the present slow pace. The barriers to a more rapid expansion of synthetic energy sources are related not to price but to environmental delays, regulatory uncertainties, and the ever-present dispute between private and public investment in these alternate energy forms. That higher prices will not induce a greater supply of synthetic energy supplies is amply demonstrated by the course of recent experience. Ten years ago the estimated cost of producing a barrel of shale oil was in the range of $5 to $7. At that time domestic crude oil cost $3 per barrel and foreign oil about $2 per barrel. It was argued then that if oil prices were to rise to the $5 to $7 per barrel range, ample supplies of shale oil could be produced. Under present government regulations oil produced from shale could receive $14 per barrel in the U.S. market, but the estimated costs are now in the $20 to $25 per barrel range. If conventional oil prices rise to the $20 to $25 per barrel range, it is likely that costs of producing oil from shale will rise to the $35 to $40 per barrel range. The only way to stop this catch-up inflation game is for government to invest in or to subsidize through price guarantees the development of these synthetic energy supplies. Since this involves only relatively small amounts of production, in the range of at most 200,000 barrels per day by 1985, a relatively modest sum would get us on the "engineering learning curves" which will ultimately lead to truly lower-cost energy supplies. But the United States need not pay ever-higher oil prices on its entire consumption of 20 million barrels per day in order to induce an incremental 200,000 barrels per day. That is sheer economic nonsense. In fact, goverment investment in synthetic oil production facilities should be viewed as part of the cost of our Strategic Petroleum Reserve, so that market prices need not be an immediate consideration in the development of an "infant industry" synthetic fuels business.

Foreign Policy

International oil issues are too frequently related to questions of U.S. foreign policy. That certain OPEC states have chosen to use their oil resources and subsequent financial wealth as weapons in the diplomatic arena is no reason for the U.S. to acquiesce in this policy. The central OPEC threat is economic, because it is a cartel whose monopoly powers are so distorting the international oil market that worldwide economic prosperity has been disrupted. OPEC member governments are sellers of oil; consuming-country governments are buyers of oil. Market interests, therefore, diverge. The United States and other important oil-consuming nations can be political allies of OPEC member states but can still forcefully negotiate with them over the price of oil. The technical plans proposed in this book are all directed toward stimulating a more effective commercial bargaining process in worldwide oil markets. These proposals should, in principle, bear little relevance to those international political questions that now cloud foreign policy perceptions concerning U.S. relations with some of the OPEC member states. Nevertheless, this linkage has been made so strong that the political implications of attempting to dilute the control of the OPEC monopoly cannot be ignored.

The key foreign policy theorem on which this linkage rests is that any attempt to confront the OPEC cartel on commercial grounds could be destabilizing to Mideast politics, particularly in the Persian Gulf. That is, if intra-OPEC frictions grow as a result of competitive pressures in the oil market, there could be increased instability in Mideastern oil-producing nations. In this volatile area of the world violence could erupt and cause serious physical damage to oil-producing and transporting facilities, thereby potentially halting the flow of oil. Or intra-OPEC frictions could even result in the overthrow of conservative, pro-Western regimes in the Persian Gulf and open up possibilities for increased Soviet influence in the area. The U.S. government, therefore, has not attempted to dilute the price-setting powers of the OPEC cartel but accepts instead the monopoly price of international oil and the continuing economic damage that it is doing. In certain sophisticated foreign policy circles the perception is that the United States probably could obtain significant decreases in the price of international oil but does not dare to let it happen. Some of the reasoning for this may be related to the misconceptions about conservation and alternate fuel supplies (alluded to in the previous section) but for the most part, the acceptance of OPEC pricing derives from this fear of political instability that would be caused by the demise of the cartel. Needless to say, the projection of a future world oil shortage fits neatly into this package of misconceptions.

The link between high oil prices and Mideastern political stability cannot be supported by historical evidence or economic logic. The sparsely populated Mideastern oil-producing nations may or may not retain their political stability, regardless of what happens to international oil prices. That is, historical conflicts in the Arab world are related to emotional and religious issues and to the aspirations of certain groups confronting an entrenched status quo. The area is a hotbed of political intrigue and potential revolution. But to relate these characteristics to the price of international oil seems to be stretching the logic to absurdity. To put it bluntly, if there is subversion of the existing Saudi Arabian regime, or if Iran is subject to continued internal disruptions, or if Iraq attacks Kuwait, none of these events will have much to do with whether oil prices are $10, $15, or $20 per barrel. These, or similar hypothetical events, could be related to the enormous wealth that these oil rich nations now possess, but that wealth derives for the most part from the massive oil reserves themselves and less so from their price. In fact, one could argue that the higher the international price, the greater the probability of political instability. In any event, I believe this linkage is more imagined than real.

Even if some minor links could be shown to exist between high oil prices and Mideastern political stability, is it worth paying the price? The economic damage done to the world economy, the threat of Eurocommunism spurred on by the high rate of unemployment among the youth of Europe, and the constraints on the independence of American foreign policy judgments all suggest that the price is too high. That is, paying high oil prices to OPEC, in the mistaken belief that the Middle East will be more stable as a result, is a very costly foreign policy judgment. At least, it deserves considerable congressional scrutiny and open debate in public forum.

Oil and the Arab-Israeli Conflict

The Arab-Israeli conflict is one of the modern world's most intractable political problems. A number of key OPEC states are party to this dispute, further complicating the issues surrounding international oil markets. Current OPEC pricing practices were created during one of the more violent episodes in the Arab-Israeli conflict and perhaps even as a result of that military confrontation. Some recounting of those events may be instructive in discerning the true nature of the link between oil and the Arab-Israeli dispute.

In October of 1973 several Arab states attacked Israel, ostensibly to recover lands lost in 1967. After initial Arab victories took a heavy toll on Israeli military equipment, the United States resupplied the Israelis, enabling them to turn the tide of battle against the Arabs. As a result of the U.S. action several Arab states who were not direct combatants in the war imposed an oil embargo on the United States (and the Netherlands). These Arab oil-producing states understood that an embargo per se could not be effective because they could not control the destination of the oil after it left their shores. As a result, they imposed a cutback on oil production that eventually amounted to about 20 percent of their normal supplies. It was this decline in oil production, not the embargo itself, that rapidly drove up the spot price of oil in Mideastern and African markets. Those OPEC countries that did not impose an embargo, some Arab and some non-Arab, sold oil at these panic prices and realized for the first time that buyers would pay substantially more than they had in the past. At the same time OPEC held a series of meetings that established their right to set oil prices unilaterally, negating all prior price commitments to the oil companies operating in their countries. The Arab countries who had in fact shut in oil production to punish the world for its support of Israel were relatively modest in their price demands, and the initial OPEC decision at that time decreed a price of about $5 per barrel, up from the prevailing $2 per barrel. Shortly thereafter OPEC met again and, under the lead of Iran and Venezuela, decided to raise the price to nearly $10 per barrel. (Subsequent events in the past five years have pushed that official price to at least $15 as of this writing.) The embargo was lifted in the spring of 1974, and oil production was restored. The price, however, remained fixed by the oil-producing countries at about five times the level that had existed only six months before.

It is apparent that at the time of the 1973 Arab-Israeli war, the sparsely populated, oil-rich Arab states in the Persian Gulf viewed the oil weapon as primarily one of withholding supplies. The drive for sharply higher prices came from the OPEC members who were indifferent to the Mideastern political situation but saw in it a major opportunity to turn the terms of trade with the West heavily in their favor and thereby substantially improve their prospects for rapid economic development. Some Arab OPEC members, who did not in fact shut in oil production, simply wanted to earn as much as they could while the bonanza lasted. There are, therefore, widely differing motives and perspectives within OPEC, and influencing the course of the Arab-Israeli conflict is only one of a number of political objectives sought by the members of the cartel.

Because of its vast oil reserves and small population Saudi Arabian influence stands out both in the councils of OPEC and by its ability to influence the diplomatic and military balance in the Arab-Israeli dispute. The Saudis are the chief exponent of the oil weapon, which today means not only the threat of oil embargo but also the threat of not increasing oil production to meet world demand, the threat of rapidly raising prices again, and more recently the threat of using their accumulated financial wealth against those who support Israel in the Mideastern political confrontation. The Saudis are extremely skillful in using this oil weapon and are careful not to employ it excessively. International diplomatic tactics require the creation of a perceived threat in order to limit the options that a potential adversary might consider using. In other words, the Saudis do not wish to so anger Western nations that they become politically estranged from them but would like to influence Western governments to pressure Israel into a position in which it will be forced to accept a potentially hostile Palestinian state on its borders. On the one hand, Saudi oil wealth requires an American presence for economic development and for military protection against potential predators; on the other hand, Saudi oil power dictates an American diplomatic tilt toward the Arab side of the Arab–Israeli dispute.

The appropriate American response to this two–sided relationship is admittedly a difficult one. A mutuality of interest does exist between the United States and Saudi Arabia: we need their oil, and they need our technical skills and military support. On the other hand, American support for Israel derives not only from a long–standing moral commitment but also from our own need to preserve the only genuinely stable, non–Communist democracy in the Mideast. Faced with this ambivalence, U.S. policymakers have been unable to frame a coherent response to both the international oil problem and its political dimensions within the context of the Arab–Israel conflict.

The perception of Saudi hegemony over future world oil supplies has dominated foreign policy attitudes since 1973. A different reading of the international oil problem would result in a different political perception of an appropriate U.S. policy role with regard to the Arab–Israeli conflict. If the United States were to adopt an international oil policy that attempted to dilute OPEC's monopoly power in the international oil market, seeking in fact to reduce international oil prices during the coming period of market surplus, then a strong, democratic Israel would become vital to U.S. interests if a split within OPEC led to increased political instability in the Mideast. That is, if intra–OPEC frictions on commercial oil policy grounds lead to a lower price for international oil and increased unrest in the Persian Gulf, then a strong Israel may be our best ally for controlling the diplomatic, economic, and military situations. How long the current regime in Saudi Arabia and the dictatorships in Iraq and Libya can last may be independent of U.S. actions anyway. The current turmoil in Iran forcefully demonstrates this point. But to the extent that commercial actions by the United States might be related to growing instability in or among the OPEC nations, the capabilities of the United States to respond to potential left-wing, Soviet-backed regimes in the Arab world might be enhanced by increasing the U.S. commitment to Israel. In other words, it is not necessarily a one-way street heading in the Arab direction, as currently perceived by some Mideastern policymakers in the U.S. government. The United States has vital interests in the security of Israel and in maintaining access to Saudi oil supplies, not only for itself but even more so for its Western European and Asian allies. Even if OPEC's monopoly price-setting powers were diluted by responsive U.S. commerical actions, the world's heavy dependence on Arab oil supplies will not change much. It is likely to diminish, but Saudi and other Arab oil will still be needed. As a result, some accommodation to the Arab position in the Arab-Israeli dispute seems inevitable, although probably not to the extent demanded by the current Arab line. A much more prosperous Middle East could ultimately emerge from a peace settlement if Israeli technological skills combine with Arab capital to develop such heavily populated and less-developed Arab nations as Egypt.

Nevertheless, the diplomatic process by which this accommodation is eventually reached need not be totally distorted by false images of Arab oil power. In 1978 the congressional debate concerning the sale of fighter planes to Saudi Arabia was an example of the perceived rather than actual threat of oil pressure. It was not the Saudis who raised the oil issues, at least not publicly. It was the Carter administration that persuaded the Senate by using the veiled arguments that the Saudis might cut their oil production, or raise oil prices, or demand payment for oil in currencies other than dollars, or even massively withdraw funds from the United States. These arguments were spurious for the simple reason that it was not in the Saudi interest to do so.

First, world oil supplies were abundant prior to the shutdown of production in Iran; when Iranian supplies return, surplus market conditions will again prevail. Saudi production in 1978 was at its lowest level in two years, and the Saudis cannot cut production much below their average 1978 levels without hurting themselves financially. Saudi production cuts would have been replaced by additional oil from the North Sea, Mexico, the North Slope of Alaska, and some of the other OPEC countries now anxious to sell more oil. Second if it had not been for the temporary loss of Iranian oil, a true price rise could not have occurred in 1979 because of this growing supply. When and if Iran returns to its historical production levels, the OPEC countries are not likely to receive the higher prices that they demand because it is unlikely that the purchasing oil companies would pay the higher prices. Third, any large move by OPEC to require payment in currencies other than the dollar is improbable if not impossible. The lack of sufficient liquidity of the currencies that they would receive would make it too costly for them. Finally, the Saudis are unlikely to dump their vast dollar holdings because of the unsettled conditions that it could cause in the financial markets. It would hurt them more than it would hurt us.

U.S. policy had little to fear in terms of Saudi reaction to a denial of the airplanes. This is not to deny Saudi Arabia the planes, if they could have been justified on truly military grounds. Saudi Arabia and the United States should be allies, and perhaps there are good reasons for selling them these aircraft. But the United States should not have been forced into such a sale on the mistaken notion that the Saudis could, or would, harm us economically if we denied them these airplanes. The relative ease with which the air-plane-sale proposal passed the Senate is indicative of the strength of the perception of Saudi dominance over world oil markets, even among a number of Israel's supporters in the Senate.

Dilution of the price-setting power of OPEC would, in my judgment, considerably alter this perceived threat of Arab oil dominance. Although Saudi and other Arab oil supplies would continue to be important in world markets, the loss of total pricing control by OPEC would significantly change the course of American diplomacy in its search for a settlement of the Arab-Israeli conflict. Under the present conditions our neutrality as a mediator is suspect by the Israelis, and we have almost no leverage with the Arabs. Whatever settlement occurs eventually should not take place as a result of the imagined rather than real political pressures resulting from OPEC control of the world's oil supplies.

American Political Will

The collapse of the Shah of Iran and the anti-Western tone of its new regime have changed the balance of power in the Mideast. As in Southeast Asia the United States may no longer be perceived in much of the Arab world as being capable of fulfilling the commitments that it undertakes. The new credo is Islamic power and contempt for the impotence of the West. The dramatic impact of the Arab oil embargo and, even more important, the colossal success of the OPEC pricing cartel is in part perceived as due to the generosity of Allah who blessed the Moslem Middle East with so much "black gold." Thus it seems that the religious values of Muhammedanism have been richly rewarded, while the hedonism of the West is suspect. This may be a new force on the world scene, far different from the Communist materialism of the Soviet Union. Technological progress and an egalitarian income distribution are not part of the Koran's teachings. Mystical faith and medieval concepts of human behavior are still the dominant principles of Islam.

This impression of Islamic power and American impotence is for the present only a delusion. If we choose to use our economic strength or our military power, we could break the oil weapon without difficulty. But our combination of postcolonial guilt and post-Vietnam paralysis has encouraged Islam to believe again in its own destiny. A modern Jihad may now be at hand, posing new and different challenges to both sides of the Iron Curtain. Islam is the dominant religion of the developing world, and the Arabs are the dominant force within Islam.

As leader of the Western world the United States must respond to this challenge. Public self-recrimination is of little value. The time may now have passed when the cautious diplomacy of the State Department and the ethical fantacies of the foreign policy establishment can maintain the status quo. The first step in responding to the economic challenge may be to demonstrate our own economic strength. If the relatively mild suggestions made in this book are insufficient, there are more powerful economic countermeasures. In the final analysis, if military intervention is required, our elected leaders should not shrink from this responsibility.

Conclusions

It is a sorry fact that world oil pricing has moved from the discipline of the marketplace to the political councils of OPEC. It is even sorrier that American businessmen, so wedded in principle to the concepts of competitive free enterprise, are now being enticed into supporting OPEC monopoly pricing of oil in their desire to sell their products to the newly rich OPEC countries. But sorriest of all are the intellectual apologists of OPEC who strain to justify OPEC's actions. A recent example is an article by Dr. Loring Allen writing in *Harvard Magazine* of May–June 1978. He states:

> The oil producing countries, it was said would never unite. When they did, they overthrew a private cartel, quintupled the crude oil price, and recycled millions to underdeveloped nations. *In the long run, we may all come out ahead.* [Italics added]

> Oil importing countries soon discovered that greater oil production and conservation, as well as successful substitutes require the protection of a high and stable oil price. Instead of a pariah, OPEC found itself the secret darling of energy planners, and its oil market a necessary condition for energy policy. OPEC, in creating an artificial shortage, has convinced the leadership of the world of the growing real scarcity of oil. How much longer supplies will last, no one knows. Known reserves used at prevailing rates may last a bit into the next century. More reserves will be found and technical advances will improve the recovery rate. But the present flood of oil will become a river, the river a stream, and the stream a trickle. And the price of oil will climb until its use for heat, power, and locomotion becomes unthinkable. OPEC is providing a breathing space during which the world can develop substitutes and adjust its life conditions to the absence of oil. By holding a price umbrella over oil, OPEC discourages wasteful consumption, stretches and develops new supplies and buys time, while sparking the introduction of substitutes. Eventually, of course, OPEC oil will disappear. In the interim OPEC serves the interests of oil importing countries by permitting an orderly and expeditious adjustment.

> Denouncing OPEC for causing the world's economic and energy ills is like blaming the messenger for bearing bad tidings. OPEC did not create the world's ravenous appetite for oil, nor did it deplete the oil reserves. It's members did, as prudent countries should, take advantage of their oil.

They created a new and stable market that saves oil and encourages substitutes in the epoch of dwindling reserves. It is now up to the industrial countries to accept the new reality, to support the oil and raw material markets, to develop new energy sources, and to sponsor a more equitable world community.

With friends like OPEC, who needs enemies? Dr. Allen's statements show very clearly the state of American international oil policy that finds it necessary to accept the scarcity thesis and pay the economic and political price. There is nothing we can do in the short run, namely, in the next twenty to thirty years. Let us proclaim impossible conservation and synthetic production goals, penalize domestic oil companies, and go along with OPEC.

The appropriate response to this rationalization of monopoly is to recognize that American diplomacy has no leverage over OPEC decisions nor over the calculations of any of its powerful members. Saudi Arabia does not need our good will, and in our own interest we must protect the Saudi oil fields against any attempt to seize them or to shut them down. But neither need we worry about Saudi displeasure. They will produce neither more oil to please us nor less oil to spite us. The Saudis and the OPEC cartel as a whole will produce and sell the amount of oil that will bring them the maximum revenues. This is not only an economic objective but also a political goal; the more income they receive, the greater is their diplomatic and military influence. There was little in the original Carter energy plan nor is there very much in the recently enacted congressional legislation that will seriously reduce the outflow of American dollars to the OPEC countries. The physical volume of imports will stay flat at best and could very well continue to rise. The only way to reduce this dollar drain for the next decade is to take direct commerical steps to counter the monopoly price set by OPEC. As Professor M.A. Adelman of MIT has often emphasized, every cartel with excess capacity is vulnerable to disruption, and the oil nations fear competitive bidding among themselves. The U.S. government should make the technical changes in the oil market that would stimulate competition among the OPEC nations.

Politically the results of taking the steps I propose would give the United States some real rather than imagined bargaining chips at the negotiating table. By imposing an import quota, the United States could allow additional or unlimited imports from favored countries. By limiting the volume of Saudi oil coming into the United States, we could be more independent of Saudi influence in helping the Egyptians and Israelis toward a durable peace. By investing in oil exploration in non–OPEC developing countries, we could reduce the political influence of the OPEC cartel on these nations in international diplomatic forums. By removing the foreign tax credit and encouraging organized market pricing for oil, we could modify some of the commerical practices of the international oil industry that lend to the cohesion of the cartel. We have been confused and fearful for five years; it is time for bolder action.

Appendix A
Domestic Energy Issues

The National Energy Plan

While the emphasis of this book is on international oil, it is clear that any steps taken by the United States toward reducing OPEC's monopoly power over world oil prices will depend heavily on a rational, domestic energy policy. Washington's energy policy is confusing; worse, existing policy is harmful, both in terms of reducing imports and keeping down real fuel costs. Modified versions of some of President Carter's April 1977 proposals were enacted by Congress in the fall of 1978. The centerpiece of this legislation was the natural gas bill, designed to deregulate the interstate price of new natural gas on a gradual basis through 1985. At the same time, intrastate gas prices have come under the regulation of the federal government for the first time. Because of this price-equalizing process, large amounts of intrastate gas have become available for consumption in the interstate market. Although the natural gas legislation is complex in terms of defining different categories of gas for pricing purposes, the legislation is likely to accomplish its major purpose in the long run, namely, to stimulate the production of new natural gas supplies, thereby alleviating at least partially the growing pressure of oil imports. The immediate deregulation of new gas from depths below fifteen thousand feet as well as from other unconventional sources (Devonian shales and geopressurized methane) also offers the prospect of reversing the decade-old decline in natural gas reserves.

The three other parts of the energy legislation are less controversial and are likely to be less substantial in their impact. The parts of the energy legislation dealing with utility-rate reform, coal conversion, and conservation will make only marginal changes in a process that the private sector is already pursuing without any directives from Washington. Utility-rate reform puts guidelines on the degree and timing of new approaches to the pricing of electricity but leaves the process of experimenting with different pricing approaches up to the states, both to the utility commissions and to the utility companies themselves. Each state must report back to the Department of Energy within two or three years with the results of the new pricing approaches. Presumably, these new approches will include time-of-day metering, peak-load pricing, and lifeline rates, all of which are now being tried by some states. Thus the legislation basically encourages a process of change that is already taking place. Since there is neither penalty nor reward involved in the legislation, its impact becomes one of communicating a sense of Congress to the rate-making authorities across the country, to the utility executives, and to the public at large.

The coal-conversion part of the legislation bans over a gradual period of time the use of oil and gas under boilers. By 1990 all utilities and industrial plants are supposed to use coal for steam generation, except where a specific exemption is granted. These exemptions may be granted to the user when he cannot obtain a reliable supply of coal or when local environmental restrictions prevent him from burning coal. This legislation is likely to speed up the private-sector response but will not materially change the vast number of state and local restrictions against the mining, transport, and burning of coal. The regulatory barriers to increasing the use of coal are primarily at the state and local levels, not at the federal level. The legislation on coal conversion does nothing to break down these barriers. In the coal-producing states labor problems prevent expansion of existing mines or environmentalist opposition prevents the opening of new mines. For Western coal especially the prospect of major new surface mines has served to arouse a negative public opinion, with images of destroyed landscapes, lack of water, and ugly railroad development. In the coal-consuming states fear of excessive air pollution continues to block efforts by utilities to increase their use of coal. Desulfurization of coal through the so-called scrubber technology is just not a practical reality in most cases at this time.

The final piece of energy legislation deals with conservation, and taxation is the primary mechanism employed to that end. Those who burn more oil and gas will pay higher taxes, those who burn less will pay lower taxes (or receive tax credits). This system is to be applied to both individuals and corporations. For individuals tax credits will be granted for insulation and for installing either more efficient or solar-related home-heating or air-conditioning systems, while a tax on gas-guzzling automobiles is planned to begin in 1980 and to increase in severity through 1985. For industrial users tax credits and accelerated depreciation will be granted for more energy-efficient equipment (including cogeneration), while these credits will be denied to industrial users who continue to install new oil and gas-fired boilers, except where these are required by local air-pollution rules. These penalties and rewards apply only to manufacturing and processing industries.

Although nuclear-fueled electrical generation will grow from about 12 percent today to almost 20 percent of electrical capacity by 1985, that represents significantly less nuclear capacity, both absolutely and relatively, than has been projected in past years. New orders for nuclear plants were at a standstill in 1978, and few if any new orders are on the horizon for 1979 and 1980. Since it takes ten to twelve years to get a large nuclear facility onstream, the outlook for capacity in 1990 and beyond is extremely uncertain. While the post 1990 outlook is far enough away to permit both natural gas and coal-based low-BTU gas to fill some of this gap, a number of critical decisions will have to be made in the near term if a serious electrical capacity shortage after 1990 is to be avoided.

The Carter administration did propose a nuclear siting bill in 1978 but little debate has taken place on this issue. Presumably, the Department of Energy will press this issue in 1979, after passage of its long-stalled comprehensive energy plan. The proposed legislation would speed up the nuclear licensing and regulatory process and would establish a "bank" of possible future sites for new nuclear plants around the country. Opposition promises to be strong, and White House support appears to be waning, so that prospects for passage in 1979 are dim.

As a commercially profitable industry solar energy is only about four years old. There are some 150 companies now engaged in both the commercial and residential solar markets, primarily in solar-heating applications. Solar tax incentives are now a part of the new energy legislation. Homeowners and renters who install solar devices will receive a tax credit of 30 percent on the first $2,000 of outlays and 20 percent of the next $8,000, for a maximum of $2,200. Businesses will receive an extra 10 percent investment tax credit for installing solar equipment. The credit is limited to 100 percent of tax liability and is refundable to the taxpayer. It applies to equipment placed in service after October 1, 1978. Coupled with a $100 million military construction bill designed to further promote solar energy, 1979 could become a landmark year for the solar business. *Business Week* devoted a major cover story to the solar business and concluded that solar was "an infant industry ready for growth."[1] Strong federal research and development support continued in 1978 and can be expected to increase in 1979. Current research and development is focusing increasingly on reducing the costs of storage, which is lagging behind advances in collection and conversion technology. This is especially true in any applications of solar electricity, where the major long-run payoffs may lie, not only for the developers but also for the national interest in reducing U.S. oil imports. Even the Electric Power Research Institute seems cautiously optimistic for the long run, although many technological and economic hurdles remain before solar electricity will become a reality.

Energy Policy Trade-Offs

No one really knows what the energy bill's net effect on the economy or on American life-styles will be. The government suggests that the economic impact will ultimately be neutral. It is the administration's hope that higher energy prices will be offset by less energy consumption, thereby keeping total energy costs from rising much more sharply in the future. The government is guessing that jobs lost in industries hurt by higher energy prices will be found in new or expanded industries providing insulation, energy-efficient equipment, and new energy sources. If, in fact, the government is right, we will all enjoy a cleaner environment and suffer no significant loss of jobs or real income. But what if the administration is wrong? What if higher fuel prices do not substantially restrain fuel consumption but simply lead to higher rates of inflation?

President Carter's energy program is a move in the right direction, but it is only a half step. It puts heavy emphasis on conservation but a low priority on increasing new energy supplies. Some fundamental choices have to be made between an energy policy that stresses conservation—as the president's does—and one that also emphasizes new supply. Those who favor conservation point out the benefits of a cleaner environment and a lower rate of economic growth. Those who favor new supplies emphasize the need for more jobs and for a higher rate of economic growth. Others see the redistribution of the economic pie as the most important element in the energy equation, stressing the need for sharing the burdens of higher energy costs more equitably and for preventing energy producers from making windfall profits from the growing resource scarcity. Still others suggest that monopoly pricing by the oil-exporting countries represents the principal cause of the energy crisis. Within these groups there are many shades of opinion, making energy one of the most divisive issues in American politics today.

There are valid elements in each of these viewpoints, and the administration has tried to incorporate many of them into its proposed national energy plan. Needless to say, the administration failed, as Congress modified substantially all the key initial proposals. Thus the broad energy policy trade-offs seem to need further explanation and discussion.

Energy and the Economy

Five years have passed since the abrupt increase in the relative price of energy. During this time the U.S. economy has experienced a sharp recession and a subsequent economic recovery. For that recovery to be sustained, the capacity to supply new goods and services will have to be increased. That increase will have to take place despite a higher relative cost of energy than in earlier periods.

The high price of energy today is causing both the cancellation of capital projects that are uneconomical and higher prices for the final outputs of those capital projects that are undertaken. The result is that the high cost of energy becomes—simultaneously—both an inflationary and a recessionary force. If business is to expand capacity, there must be a reasonable expectation that the output can be sold at prices high enough to yield an acceptable return on investment. The capital projects that are being postponed or cancelled are delivering neither the jobs nor the increased productivity needed in an expanding economy.

These energy-related distortions have blunted the conventional tools of economic policy. The twin evils of unemployment and inflation do not respond readily to conventional monetary and fiscal policies. It would help to supplement them with policies that encourage capital spending—in particular, spending on energy-related projects that would conserve energy or increase energy supply and that would be economically justified. Government economic policy needs to maintain the incentives for profitable private investment in an economy where the distortions of the energy crisis join a growing list of social and environmental costs that business must pay. Without such private investment the prospects for increasing the employment base of the U.S. economy in a noninflationary manner are bleak.

The relationship between energy and employment is such that it takes more and more energy to supply a job at the level of productivity we have come to expect from the U.S. economy. Increased energy use is a prerequisite to the increased capital intensity of the U.S. employment structure. Increased energy intensity makes for increased labor productivity and consequently for the gains in real income that we call prosperity. Thus our prosperity is based on a high per capita energy consumption; we require large amounts of energy to produce the goods and services that give us a high standard of living.

The historical growth of the economy suggests that the increases in energy consumption and in productive employment are jointly related to the growth of output. Output must grow faster than employment to generate increased productivity and real per capita income gains. But if output does grow materially faster than employment, so will energy use. Despite the dramatic shift in employment away from manufacturing and capital-intensive industries generally, the consumption of energy per productive job has continued to increase as an integral part of the process of capital formation.[2]

We are faced with the dual problems of unemployment and excessive dependence on foreign sources of energy. Yet we have been unable to weld together an effective employment and energy policy. Solutions will be neither quick nor easy. But the longer we delay, the greater the vulnerability of many American jobs to foreign economic and political pressures. Between now and 1985 it is likely that the U.S. dependence on foreign oil will not decrease from its present high level. The advent of the Alaskan pipeline has only temporarily arrested the decline in U.S. oil production, while delays in increased coal production and nuclear power will have to be compensated for through increased oil imports. While we have imposed restrictions on rising domestic energy costs, we must still pay the price internationally. Imported oil that had been costing us $7 billion to $8 billion annually before the 1973 embargo now costs $50 billion. The more time we waste in resolving our domestic energy supply problem, the more oil we will have to import from OPEC at what will likely be ever-rising prices. In 1978 the United States spent about $45 billion for imported energy, an amount equal to our capital investment in domestic production of energy. Compare that to 1962, when the United States invested about $10 billion in domestic energy while paying $1.8 billion for energy imports. In fifteen years our spending on imported energy has grown from less than 20 percent to almost 100 percent of our domestic energy investments.

A proportion of the resources devoted to importing oil could be fruitfully invested in increasing the supply of U.S. energy and in creating productive employment. Replacing U.S. oil imports with an equivalent amount of domestic energy would generate many productive new jobs in the United States, depending on the particular policies adopted. Some of these new jobs could come from additional domestic energy production and from the construction of new plant facilities. The balance of new growth in employment would be derived from nonenergy sectors, which would produce more goods and services both to support the energy-producing industries and to supply what would become a generally faster-growing economy. Although the policy alternatives to achieve these improved employment opportunities may differ, the overall implication for the economy is the same: idle manpower can be put to work in the implementation of a policy of greater energy self-sufficiency.

Energy and the Environment

Being for a clean environment is as much a cliche as being for motherhood and apple pie. But decisions have to be made about priorities. The extreme environmentalist position questions the need for continued economic growth, arguing that we would all be healthier and happier with a slower pace of economic activity. While this utopian vision of society might appeal to a narrow segment of American public opinion, it is not a viable option in a world of competing claims on limited resources. Intergroup frictions would be exacerbated by a stagnating economy.

The more pertinent question is how to reconcile the widespread concern for a cleaner environment with the need for economic growth. The Carter program suggests that we can use less energy as we produce and consume the goods and services that make for a healty economy. According to the administration, the use of less energy per unit of output will help to preserve the environment while still maintaining a viable economy.

The tough trade-offs, however, are quantitative. How far can we go in one direction without jeopardizing the goals of the other? There are no simple answers, but a few observations might be helpful.

First, we have imposed many new environmental regulations without recognizing the increased costs of meeting these new standards. Energy costs have risen not only because the resources themselves have become scarce but also because the techniques for producing and consuming these resources must now meet tougher environmental standards than in the past. At the same time energy consumers have an understandably negative reaction to paying the higher prices that result from these increased costs. By proposing higher taxes on energy use, the government is not only sending us a signal that we need to reduce fuel consumption but also telling us that we have to pay for the cost of maintaining a cleaner environment. Second, it is important to remember that because energy investments require very long lead times before any new production is available, the energy-producing industries need a consistent, long-term set of guidelines that they can be reasonably sure will be applicable at the time a new plant comes on-stream. Indecision in Washington concerning the energy-environment trade-off and the constantly changing pattern of regulations have delayed new investment. President Carter's policy statement recognizes this issue and states: "Reasonable certainty and stability in government policies are needed to enable consumers and producers of energy to make investment decisions."

Finally, nationwide environmental standards may be inappropriate, since it is the local community that must pay for the higher costs of a clean environment and make the decisions concerning the potential loss of jobs and income. Regional differences are significant, and local autonomy in the environment-energy trade-off should be preserved as much as possible.

Energy and Equity

Since the American people became aware of the energy crisis, there has been widespread resentment against the oil industry for allegedly profiting unwarrantedly from the high oil prices imposed by the oil-exporting nations. As a result, the need to share the burden of sacrifice equally between oil companies and their customers has become a constant theme of national energy policy. The former Republican administration followed this theme when it proposed a windfall-profits tax and the use of compensating payments to low-income groups as part of its attempt to decontrol U.S. crude-oil prices. The present Democratic administration follows this theme, too; it is keenly aware of the political barriers to allowing the revenues from higher oil prices to flow back to the oil producers. To quote President Carter: "If producers were to receive tomorrow's prices for yesterday's discoveries, there would be an inequitable transfer of income from the American people to the producers, whose profits would be excessive and would bear little relation to actual economic contribution" (April, 1977).

The administration's proposal for dealing with this equity issue and at the same time for forcing the public to pay the higher international price in the interest of conservation was to impose a tax on the difference between the present regulated U.S. price and the world price—the crude-oil wellhead tax. The revenues from this tax, which could be as high as $15 billion annually when fully implemented, would be rebated to the public in form of income tax credits. The administration claimed that this approach would recycle these funds through the economy in a more equitable manner than the distribution arrived at through conventional private transactions. Unfortunately, higher taxes will not buy us one additional drop of domestic oil, whereas market prices for oil would inevitably stimulate domestic supply. The government's program would not induce much conservation either, since the final price paid by the consumer would not be much higher than it is now.

It is a simple truth of resource economics that when incremental supplies become scarce, those who own existing and less expensive supplies stand to make windfall profits. If these profits are reinvested in additional productive facilities, they serve a useful purpose. To the extent that they are not reinvested, however, taxing them away would be appropriate. It would be logical (and easy) to devise a program to encourage reinvestments of these profits in new productive facilities by taxing the portion that is not reinvested. Instead the federal government proposed to preempt any such windfalls and donate them to the consumer through a complicated scheme of wealth redistribution. This raised substantial controversy, concerned less with energy than with our tax and welfare goals. As such it was defeated in Congress.

Conclusions

I would like to quote Robert Roosa, a prominent New York banker:

> It is becoming increasingly evident, whatever the original merits of the OPEC case might have been, that the mutation of energy costs which occurred in late 1973 has in fact drastically altered the "production function" of the world economy, apparently imposing a slower or lower gradient for overall growth than might otherwise have been attainable. And until comprehensive new energy policies are devised and implemented, here and abroad, the non-OPEC nations will continue for some years ahead to confront that real obstacle to higher growth, while also suffering the consequences of a disequilibrium in their trading relations with each other— even without another round of oil price increases. In these circumstances, while traditional monetary and fiscal tools will help further cyclical recovery they may not be enough to sustain that recovery, and are quite inadequate to repair the critical structural distortion that has occurred. Nor can conservation strategies by themselves provide an answer to the structural problem, unless we are willing to sacrifice even more growth and prolong unemployment. A full recovery requires that deliberate action of a far bolder character be undertaken.[3]

Mr. Roosa then goes on to outline a long-term plan of action in which government and business could participate jointly in the implementation of programs designed to achieve a greater degree of energy self-reliance.

The partnership of business and government has a number of precedents, especially in the postwar economic experience of the United States. Both the development of synthetic rubber and the founding of the aerospace industry were joint responses by government and business to critical national problems. The energy crisis today demands no less attention than the challenges of World War II and of the Soviet Sputnik crisis. With the bitterness of Vietnam and Watergate behind us, the political climate is now more amenable to the development of an acceptable national energy program built around a successful partnership of private industry and of sound public policy. Let's get on with the job.

Notes

1. "The Coming Boom in Solar Energy," *Business Week,* October 9, 1978.

2. For a fuller explanation of the energy, GNP, and employment relationships, see Arnold Safer, "Employment and Energy Independence," *Business Economics,* September 1976.

3. Brown Bros., and Harriman, New York City; report dated November 1976, based on a speech by Mr. Roosa. Reprinted by permission.

Appendix B
Status of the Foreign
Tax Credit Issue

In 1978, the U.S. Treasury issued certain rulings pertaining to the additional use of foreign tax credits by major oil companies on their operations abroad. At this time, the status of those rulings is unclear, primarily because of two unresolved issues. The first relates to the use of posted versus market prices in claiming foreign tax credits. The second involves "retroactivity," since some oil companies have accumulated a vast amount of prior tax credits due to their sale of former concession properties to OPEC host governments. In particular, those companies negotiated a system of compensation by the host governments that minimizes their capital-gains tax liabilities to the U.S. government. In some cases the companies received OPEC host-country bonds that were redeemable only against minimum levels of oil purchases by the companies from the host countries. As a result, the companies have become even more tied to lifting oil from these OPEC countries, because if they did not meet the purchase requirements, the value of the bonds would be diminished. If the Internal Revenue Service rulings were made retroactive prior to the time when these bonds were issued, the companies would lose the foreign tax creditability associated with tax liabilities resulting from the sale of the former concession properties. The bonds, or other arrangements, would then have less aftertax value for the companies and would serve to further dilute the preferred-access arrangements between the companies and the OPEC host governments.

The material which follows contains a series of direct quotes from the current Washington debate over these issues.

Introduction

The Commerce, Consumer, and Monetary Affairs Subcommittee conducted an investigation and held hearings into the effectiveness and efficiency of the Treasury Department's and the Internal Revenue Service's (IRA) handling of tax rulings related to foreign tax credits claimed by U.S. petroleum companies operating abroad. The subcommittee's study focused on the following questions: (1) Did Treasury and IRS properly administer those sections of the Tax Code relating to foreign tax credits claimed by U.S. petroleum companies operating abroad; (2) to what extent were such private tax rulings influenced by and/or coordinated with the Treasury Department's Tax Policy Division and other government entities responsible for devising U.S. energy and foreign policies; and (3) were IRS's rulings consistent with the procedural and substantive requirements of U.S. tax laws, including audit requirements of tax returns relying on such rulings. Hearings were held on September 26 and 27, October 4, and November 29, 1977.

Foreign tax credits claimed by U.S. petroleum companies cost the U.S. Treasury (as described below) over $1.2 billion annually.[1] The aggregate loss since 1974 exceeds $7 billion; and the total loss since petroleum companies began claiming tax credits in 1950 is $14 billion.[2]

The key substantive issue, which IRS first addressed in a 1955 tax ruling, is whether a petroleum company's payments to a foreign country for the right to extract petroleum located in and owned by that country is a royalty or income tax payment. If it is a royalty, then the amount is deductible as an ordinary and necessary business expense. On the other hand, under sections 901–907 of the Tax Code, a company is given a direct credit against U.S. taxes for any "income tax" payment made to a foreign government. Consequently, if a payment to a foreign government is deemed to be an "income tax" instead of a royalty, the tax benefits are considerably more valuable to the company, subject to certain quantitative limitations placed on a petroleum company's use of foreign tax credits by the Tax Reform Act of 1976. All payments by petroleum producers operating in the United States and Canada to the mineral landowner or excise taxes to local governments are considered a royalty and merely deducted as normal business expense.

The issue of foreign tax credits for petroleum companies began in 1950 when the Saudi Arabian Government sought more revenue from its oil properties and, after consultation with American oil and tax experts, decided to levy an "income tax" on Aramco (the sole producer in Saudi Arabia) in lieu

Committee on Government Operations, U.S. House of Representatives, *Foreign Tax Credits Claimed by U.S. Petroleum Companies,* Report No. 95–1240, 95th Congress, 2d sess., June 1, 1978.

of increasing its royalty for oil extractions.[3] At that time, Aramco requested a ruling from IRS that the payments made to Saudi Arabia would in fact be a creditable income tax under section 901. If such a ruling was granted, Aramco would be economically unaffected by any increase in Saudi oil revenue since the effect would be merely to shift the company's tax liability dollar-for-dollar from the United States to Saudi Arabia.

The Secretary of the Treasury's office wrote four major memoranda from 1951 to 1954 emphatically opposing a favorable ruling on the ground that the payment was in fact an increased royalty exacted in the guise of an income tax.[4] Treasury complained that the Saudi tax scheme was a "sham", the sole purpose of which was to increase Saudi revenues at the expense of the U.S. Treasury with no effect on the taxpaying oil company. In 1954 and 1955 the State Department and National Security Council intervened and, for foreign policy reasons, requested that a favorable ruling be issued so that the Saudi Government could receive additional revenues.[5] Consequently, a favorable retroactive ruling was issued in 1955[6] with a resultant loss to the U.S. Treasury of approximately $50 million for the 1950 tax year alone.[7] Other petroleum producing countries soon followed the Aramco-Saudi Arabia precedent with increasing losses to the U.S. Treasury.

Findings

1. IRS's decisions permitting U.S. petroleum companies operating abroad to claim foreign tax credits in lieu of deductions has cost the U.S. Treasury over $7 billion since 1974.

2. (a) By the early 1970's, multinational petroleum companies were operating abroad under a set of factual and legal circumstances completely at variance with those upon which the previous foreign tax credit rulings were based. As a consequence, companies claiming foreign tax credits after 1973 could not legitimately rely on the previous rulings.

(b) IRS failed to effectively examine tax returns which relied on such private rulings to determine whether the facts upon which the tax return claims were based conformed to the factual and legal requirements which formed the bases of the earlier ruling.

(c) IRS also failed to require companies relying on the previous rulings to meet the burden of proof required, to demonstrate the application of the ruling to their situation.

3. (a) On July 14, 1976, the IRS issued a press release which put companies on notice that tax credits could not be claimed for foreign "tax" payments which did not meet certain specified criteria. IRS' purpose in issuing this press release was to establish a benchmark date to which subsequent IRS rulings on foreign tax credit claims could be made retroactive.

(*b*) Notwithstanding the July 14, 1976, press release, Treasury officials urged the IRS not to make its ruling retroactive, but to delay the effective date for most companies until January 1, 1979.

(*c*) On January 16, 1978, IRS issued a ruling—to become effective for taxable years beginning on or after July 1, 1978—that prohibited U.S. petroleum companies from taking a credit for foreign payment unless certain specified criteria were met.

(*d*) The loss to the U.S. Treasury from such tax credit claims accruing from July 14, 1976, will amount to over $2 billion.

4. Despite past criticism of interference by Government agencies concerned with foreign policy in the 1955 tax ruling, the State Department and Treasury's Office of International Affairs have continued their efforts to influence the administration of the Tax Code as it relates to foreign income tax credits claimed by U.S. petroleum companies operating in (OPEC) Organization of Petroleum Exporting Countries.

5. Treasury's review of IRS' decision to revoke the 1955 Saudi Arabian and 1968 Libyan tax rulings was completely duplicative of the work done by IRS and added nothing to the initial decision. Treasury's review delayed revocation of these rulings and threatened to cause postponement of their issuance for several years more.

Treasury, in fact, did not announce its intent to rescind the prior erroneous rulings until congressional investigations demonstrated improper administration of the foreign tax credits sections of the Tax Code.

6. IRS has failed to make public, as required under section 6110(d) of the Internal Revenue Code of 1954, as amended, notations of communications with Treasury and other non-IRS government personnel concerning foreign tax credit revenue rulings or related written tax determinations.

7. A taxpayer has standing to contest any IRS decision which results in a larger tax obligation for him. However, citizens have no legal standing to challenge a possibly erroneous IRS decision which decreases another taxpayer's tax obligation despite the fact that the erroneous decision may place the citizen's business in a competitive or other disadvantage, or may cost the Treasury revenue.

8. Paragraph (f) of section 6103 of the Internal Revenue Code of 1954, as amended, which restricts disclosure of tax returns and tax return information to most congressional committees, seriously impedes congressional oversight responsibility to examine the effectiveness and efficiency of IRS' practices and procedures and to evaluate the impact of the tax laws on public policy issues. IRS and Treasury have used section 6103 (f) to deny congressional committees access to documents which could call into question the propriety of certain actions by these agencies.

Recommendations

1. (*a*) The Secretary of the Treasury should take immediate administrative action, including the promugation of written rules, regulations and guidelines, to insure that the Internal Revenue Service is free of improper influence from Government agencies which are not responsible for administration of the tax laws.

(*b*) Agencies of the Government which are not responsible for tax administration should be prohibited from attempting to influence IRS administrative rulings concerning the administration of the tax laws.

(*c*) IRS and Treasury should take immediate steps to insure that all communications to the IRS and Treasury from other Government agencies regarding written determinations by IRS be made available for public inspection as required by section 6110(d).

(*d*) The appropriate legislative committees and executive branch agencies should examine the desirability for and feasibility of making the Internal Revenue Service a separate and independent agency.

2. The Federal Rules of Civil Procedure should be amended to allow private citizens standing to obtain judicial review before U.S. District Courts of Treasury and IRS rules and regulations pertaining to other taxpayers if they place that citizen or taxpayer's business in a competitive or other disadvantage, or cost the Treasury revenues.

3. Clause 2 of Rule X of the Rules of the House of Representatives specifically grants to the Government Operations Committee general oversight responsibility to "review and study on a continuing basis, the operations of Government activities at all levels with a view to determining their economy and efficiency." In order to enable the Government Operations Committee to carry out its oversight responsibilities for IRS, section 6103(f) (1) of title 26 of the U.S. Code should be amended to read in full:

(*f*) *Disclosure to committees of Congress.* —
(1) Committee on Ways and Means, Committee on Government Operations, Committee on Finance, Committee on Governmental Affairs, and Joint Committee on Taxation.—Upon written request from the chairman of the Committees on Ways and Means or Government Operations of the House of Representatives, the chairman of the Committees on Finance or Governmental Affairs of the Senate, or the chairman of the Joint Committee on Taxation, the Secretary shall furnish such committee with any return or return information specified in such request, except that any return or return information which can be associated with, or otherwise identify, directly or indirectly, a particular taxpayer shall be furnished to such committee only when sitting in closed executive session unless such taxpayer otherwise consents in writing to such disclosure.

4. IRS should revoke its decision to postpone the effective date of Revenue Ruling 78-63.

5. IRS should seek to recover, to the extent to which it is entitled, all revenues lost as a result of foreign tax credits improperly claimed by U.S. petroleum companies.

6. IRS should devote greater resources to monitoring tax returns which rely on and benefit substantially from revenue rulings (such as tax returns which relied on foreign tax credit rulings) to ensure that the actual facts and circumstances upon which the return is based are consistent with the assumed facts upon which the ruling was granted.

Retroactivity

IRS rulings or regulations are usually deemed to apply retroactively. Section 7805(b) of the Internal Revenue Code gives the Secretary Power in special circumstances to limit the retroactive application of a ruling or regulation and to apply them prospectively. This section states:

> The Secretary or his delegate may prescribe the extent, if any, to which any ruling or regulation, relating to the internal revenue laws, shall be applied without retroactive effect.

While the Secretary may deny retroactive application of a ruling, once a ruling is issued, he should not postpone the effective date of the ruling where the ruling or regulation has been under review and the parties have been given notice of the review. Thus the postponed effective date of the recently issued foreign tax credit rulings is another extra-legal act that will permit petroleum companies to continue illegal tax credit claims.

Relief under § 7805(b) is usually granted when a taxpayer justifiably relied on a prior IRS ruling, regulation or opinion and a change in IRS' position would increase the taxpayer's liability.[8] To be eligible, the tax-payer's activities must be totally within the factual parameters of the prior rulings or regulation and such ruling or regulation must represent a change in IRS policy as opposed to a correction of a prior mistaken interpretation of the tax code.[9]

By 1976, the facts under which U.S. petroleum companies claimed foreign tax credits bore no relation to those upon which the original 1955 ruling was issued. When the initial ruling was issued, posted prices were not utilized in determining the Saudi Arabian tax base; instead the tax was based on actual receipts from the sale of oil, which is consistent with the principles of taxing only net income under U.S. income tax laws. Further-more, a tax based on a fixed per-barrel posted price is more like a royalty and not a separately calculated income tax. In fact, use of posted prices in determining the tax base was the primary reason stated by the IRS for revoking the former ruling.

Income received by petroleum companies is no longer determined on the basis of arm's-length transactions governed by marketplace considerations—another salient factor in determining foreign tax creditability. Since the 1973 oil embargo, oil companies have ceased bargaining over posted prices which are now unilaterally dictated by the OPEC cartel. Thus, an entirely different set of circumstances existed in 1973—circumstances which contravened the factors upon which the 1955 ruling was based. By 1973, there was no ruling on point with the existing facts; oil companies, which have the burden of demonstrating the application of any ruling,[10] could not justify reliance on the earlier rulings since they were based on differenct facts which were not relevant to the oil trade of 1973. Even without revocation of the prior rulings, the petroleum companies had no right to rely on them, and should have sought a new ruling to cover the radically changed circumstances.

U.S. petroleum companies had been put on notice as early as 1973 that the Service questioned the continued validity of foreign tax credits. The audits of the 19 petroleum companies with assets in excess of $250 million who have claimed foreign tax credits since 1972 have not been completed. IRS indicated that many of these audits have being held in abeyance because of questions raised regarding the legitimacy of foreign tax credits claimed, and that three of the audits, in fact, "for the 1973 tax year are being held in abeyance *solely* because of foreign tax credit issues".[11] (Italic added.) Furthermore, in 1976 revenue agents raised questions with taxpayers and made requests for technical advice with the Service's National Office regarding the legitimacy of foreign tax credits claimed by petroleum companies.[12] Because their tax returns were held in abeyance and revenue agents were raising questions regarding the interpretation and application of the tax laws to foreign tax credits claimed, the petroleum companies were well aware the IRS questioned the validity of these claims. Therefore, any petroleum company continuing to claim foreign tax credits after 1973 did so at its own risk and not in reliance on prior tax credit ruling which were not on point.

Finally, on July 14, 1976, IRS issued a news release which for the first time affirmatively stated "the specific circumstances under which a foreign tax credit would be allowed against U.S. income tax under section 901 of the Internal Revenue Code where a levy is imposed by a foreign government owning minerals extracted by U.S. taxpayers.[13] After listing a set of criteria discussed on p. 7, supra, the release stated:

> The purpose of this News Release is to state the *current* IRS position regarding a levy imposed by a foreign government owning minerals extracted

by U.S. taxpayers, in which all the characteristics above are present. Any
departure from these characteristics *may jeopardize the qualification of
the levy as a creditable income tax.* [Italic added.]

Thus, as of July 14, 1976, the entire public was aware that the Service had
established a firm set of guidelines governing foreign tax credits, and oil
companies operating within OPEC countries understood that foreign levies
on their operations did not qualify as a creditable income tax.

One former IRS official[15] indicated to the subcommittee staff that the
News Release was issued to have the impact of a general public ruling
setting forth IRS' position on foreign tax credits, and enable IRS to recover
revenue lost from illegitimate foreign tax credit claims at least as far back
as July 14, 1976. The arguments of taxpayers, Treasury's Office of International Affairs and the State Department for denying retroactive effect
were, at best, weak and the grounds for such denials were nonexistent. By
not giving the January 16, 1978, foreign tax credit ruling retroactive effect,
IRS was not only failing to enforce the tax laws, but it nullified the work of
the previous administration to reserve the right to recover revenues at least
after July 14, 1976. Failure to give the 1978 ruling its proper retroactive
application was inconsisten with a zealous administration of the tax laws to
which IRS supposedly is dedicated.

Private Actions

There is an inherent inbalance in IRS' handling of tax rulings and administration involving major issues. When the Government rules erroneously
against a taxpayer, that taxpayer quite naturally can plead his case to either
the Tax Court of the U.S. district courts. However, when Treasury and IRS
err in favor of a taxpayer or fail to effectively administer any provision of
the tax code, the general public has no recourse to correct the damage.
Moreover, errors in favor of one segment of an industry of the economy
may place a competing sector at a competitive disadvantage, but that sector
will have no remedy to correct the damage.

For example, allowing tax credits for foreign royalty payments labeled
as an income tax provides added incentive to explore and produce abroad at
the expense of domestic production. Multinational petroleum companies
have naturally invested their limited capital in those areas where they
achieve the highest rate of after–tax return. To the extent that foreign tax
credits in lieu of royalty deductions benefits these companies, the Government is providing an incentive to invest in OPEC countries which is not provided for domestic operations.[16] In fact, according to State and Treasury
memoranda, the 1976 Indonesian ruling denying creditable treatment to
that country's levy on oil production caused a significant deferral of explo-

ration capital from Indonesia to other countries.[17] Thus, it is evident that without these credits, companies will make their production and exploration decision on the basis of which areas have the greatest economic and productive possiblities—influenced less by the economic distortions of tax advantages.

Furthermore, these credits place solely domestic producers who are not internationally integrated at a competitive disadvantage vis-a-vis multi-nationals. The latter are granted credits for what are really normal business expenses which are not available to domestic producers.[18]

In June 1974 Tax Analysts and Advocates and the owner of a small independent petroleum production company brought an action seeking a declaratory judgment that the 1955 and 1969 IRS foreign tax credit rulings were unlawful and asking for an injunction requiring the Service to withdraw them.[19] Tax Advocates and Analysts has over 175 members, most of whom are tax professors and practitioners. One of its stated goals is to ensure that the IRS does not grant special interest groups unduly favorable tax treatment beyond that which the Service may lawfully provide. The District Court for the District of Columbia consluded that both petitioners lacked standing as Federal taxpayers because they had suffered no judicially cognizable injury. It went on to state that although one petitioner who owned a small domestic oil producing facility suffered injury in fact as a competitor dealing in oil extraction and production, he had no standing to sue because he could not be eligible for foreign tax credit benefit.[20] The Supreme Court refused to review the opinion.[21] Thus, the court's position is that a party, regardless of damages suffered, who would not be eligible to benefit from rulings under a particular section of the Tax Code, had no standing to object to the erroneous administration of the tax laws which favorably affect a competitor's tax liability. Needless to say, the courts have stated that in the absence of a congressional mandate, the general public has no standing to object to the erroneous administration of the tax laws despite the added financial burdens and deficits caused thereby. Consequently, IRS decisions which may add to Treasury revenues can be reviewed by the courts, but a decision which loses revenues cannot be reviewed.

Revenue Ruling 78-63: Disallowance of Credit for Taxes Paid to Saudi Arabia*

The Treasury Department today announced the issuance of three Internal Revenue Service Revenue rulings concerning the credits that U.S. businesses may take against their U.S. income taxes for taxes paid to foreign countries.

One of these rulings concluded that amounts received by Libya from

---

Treasury Press Release, Jan 16, 1978.

U.S. oil companies operating in that country are not foreign income taxes and therefore may not be credited against U.S. income taxes. Today's ruling revokes an inconsistent 1968 ruling involving Libya.

Today's ruling also revokes a 1955 IRS ruling on the basis of which payments to Saudi Arabia under a posted price system have been treated as income taxes that may be credited by U.S. oil companies against their U.S. income taxes.

The ruling issued today will take effect for taxes paid or accrued by the companies in their taxable years beginning after June 30, 1978. When an IRS ruling is revoked, the general rule is that the revocation takes effect only for the future. Revocations are not retroactive because taxpayers are entitled to rely on an IRS ruling until the IRS concludes that the ruling is no longer valid.

A principal basis for the conclusion of the ruling is the use of posted prices in computing the companies' tax payments. "Posted prices" are an arbitrary price which exceeds the market price of oil. They have been used to determine the oil companies' income, raising their nominal income and their foreign tax liabilities above the levels that would result from actual market prices.

The IRS has recently received advice that Saudi Arabia may no longer use posted prices in determining taxpayer liability. The IRS has not received detailed disclosure of all relevant information as the the current system employed by Saudi Arabia and has not been asked to determine the effect that revocation of the 1955 ruling will have on foreign tax credits claimed under a system not involving posted prices.

Foreign income taxes may be credited against income taxes owed to the United States. In determining whether a foreign tax qualifies as an income tax that can be credited against U.S. taxes, the U.S. Supreme Court has held that U.S. standards apply. The IRS ruling finds the Libyan and Saudi Arabian taxes have been in conflict with important U.S. standards of when a foreign tax may be used as a credit:

> The purpose of a foreign income tax must be to reach "net gain" and the tax must be structured so as to be almost certain of doing so. Thus, a foreign levi is not an income tax as defined under United States standards if it is intentionally structured to tax artificial or fictitious income, as is the case with tax systems that use mechanisms such as the posted price.
>
> A foreign tax can be credited only if it is imposed on income that is "realized." Income under the Libyan system is not "realized" within the mean ing of this standard since taxes are imposed even if sales are not made.

Under the ruling issued today, payments under the posted price system could be deducted from gross income in determining income subject ot U.S. tax. Before today's ruling, such payments offset, dollar for dollar, taxes the companies would have owed to the United States.

For example, assume that on $100 of taxable income by U.S. standards the U.S. tax is $48 and the tax paid to a foreign government is $85. Prior to the ruling, the foreign tax credit would fully offset the U.S. tax of $48 (and leave an excess credit of $37, which could be used against U.S. tax on other lower-taxed oil extraction income from foreign sources, if any). After the ruling takes effect, the U.S. tax would be 48 percent of $15 (100–85) or $7.2, compared to a tax of zero before today's ruling.

Under the conditions that have prevailed in the past, the use of a credit rather than a deduction for amounts paid by U.S. oil companies to Libya and Saudi Arabia resulted in tax benefits of approximately $600 million in 1976, the most recent year for which data is available. The revocation of the ruling does not imply that the amount of such tax beneftis will necessarily be eliminated or reduced. That determination cannot be made without full information about the foreign tax laws that will apply to actual operations in taxpayer fiscal years beginning after June 30, 1978. Also, it is not known if the affected companies could reorganize to avoid the effect of the revocation.

Although it is not now known if any tax increase will result from the revocation of the 1955 and 1968 rulings, if there were such an increase, it could be absorbed by the oil companies or by the producing countries or passed on in the form of higher product prices. The increase in gasoline prices attibutable to the maximum conceivable tax increase would be less than one-tenth of a cent per gallon.

Additional Views of Hon. Robert F. Drinan

The investigation by the Commerce, Consumer and Monetary Affairs Subcommittee into the Internal Revenue Service's administration of tax rulings pertaining to foreign tax credits claimed by U.S. petroleum companies revealed a long history of improper influence exerted on the IRS by the Departments of State and Treasury. In addition, the subcommittee's investigation demonstrated a continuing pattern of reluctance by the IRS to reconsider its 1955 Revenue Ruling granting foreign tax credits to petroleum companies, despite changes in circumstances so drastic as to virtually compel a reappraisal of the validity of this ruling.

Testimony and interoffice memoranda revealed that the initial 1955 ruling itself was largely the result of foreign policy concerns transmitted to the Internal Revenue Service by the Department of State and the National Security Council. Despite criticism of the 1955 ruling and the improper pressure exerted on the IRS during its formulation, the Department of State and the Department of the Treasury's Office of International Tax Policy continued their efforts to influence the Internal Revenue Service to continue its treatment of foreign oil taxes as taxes rather than royalties, in spite of the questionable 1955 ruling and subsequent "tax" increases which made these levies even more clearly royalties, rather than taxes.

The committee report clearly documents the improper influence exerted on the Internal Revenue Service, the failure of the IRS to fulfill its responsibility to carefully examine the foreign tax credit and to consider on the merits the use of that credit by the petroleum companies, the billions of dollars in revenue lost to the U.S. Treasury, and the failure of the IRS to make public, under section 6110(d) of the Internal Revenue Code, notations of communications with the Treasury Department and others concerning the foreign tax credit revenue rulings.

I would like to focus briefly upon two of the committee's recommendations, both of which constitute statutory proposals whose need is demonstrated by this report and the hearings from which it is drawn. In addition, I would like to underscore the recommendation that the Internal Revenue Service should revoke its decision to postpone the effective date of Revenue Ruling 78–63 and should apply the ruling denying the foreign tax credit to petroleum companies retroactively, so as to recover those revenues to which it is entitled.

The long history of the use of the foreign tax credit by the petroleum companies exemplifies the need for statutory change to permit taxpayers to bring suit against the Internal Revenue Service to challenge allegedly lenient tax rulings. The courts have made it clear that, absent such statutory change, taxpayers have no standing to contest such IRS rulings in court. While the detailed investigation of the use of the foreign tax credit conducted by the Government Operations Committee resulted in a reversal of the treatment of such credits, we cannot always rely on congressional action to redress erroneous IRS rulings. Courts have the capacity to remedy excessively lenient rulings expeditiously, while congressional action, whether by amendment of the IRS Code or by hearings and reports, is generally time consuming.

Conferring upon taxpayers the right to sue the IRS for lenient rulings in cases not directly involving themselves would help to counter the improper, politically based influence on the formulation of tax rulings which we documented in the petroleum companies use of the foreign tax credit. The creation of such a right would help to recover revenues improperly denied the U.S. Treasury. It would also redress a serious imbalance in the review of our tax determination, while IRS rulings which are arguably too severe will almost certainly be challenged in court by one or more of the affected parties, rulings (such as the petroleum companies use of the foreign tax credit) which are arguably too lenient will escape judicial scrutiny altogether. With proper provisions for notice, joinder and intervention, and safeguards against frivolous suits, the creation of a right to sue the IRS for lenient rulings would be an entirely positive addition to the means by which the administration and interpretation of our tax laws are conducted. I have introduced legislation which would establish this right, and I hope that the findings and recommendations of this report and the unfortunate history of the use of the foreign tax credit by the giant petroleum coporations will serve as a stimulus to the enactment of legislation to permit judicial review of allegedly lenient tax rulings. Based upon the investigation conducted by the subcommittee, the U.S. Treasury may be losing billions of dollars of revenue to which it is entitled, and access by taxpayers to the courts could most expeditiously lead to the recovery of these revenues.

The committee report also recommends that the appropriate legislative committees and the executive branch examine the necessity for and feasibility of making the Internal Revenue Service a separate and independent agency. I believe that the need for an independent IRS is clear and that the creation of such an independent agency should not pose any serious administrative problems.

This report documents the extent to which the IRS is subject to improper interference by its parent agency, the Department of Treasury. Such interference is by no means uncommon. The administration and enforcement of the Federal tax laws should be removed from political concerns to the maximum feasible extent. It seems self-evident that an independent IRS would be better able to resist outside pressure and discharge its duties impartially, as the law requires. I have introduced legislation to make the Internal Revenue Service an independent agency, and I hope that the appropriate committees will, as the committee recommends in its report, consider the establishment of such an agency.

The decision of the Internal Revenue Service to postpone the effective date of its revenue ruling denying the use of the foreign tax credit to petroleum companies is clearly unwarranted. I would like to express my wholehearted support for the committee's conclusion that failure to give the January 16, 1978 ruling full retroactive effect is completely inconsistent with the vigorous enforcement of the tax laws to which the IRS is putatively dedicated.

The postponement of the ruling's effect goes beyond the authority of the IRS. While the Secretary may deny the retroactive application of a ruling, he has no statutory authority to postpone its effective date. The larger issue of retroactivity also finds the Internal Revenue Service on this ice. According to the statute, retroactive application of a ruling is to be granted when a taxpayer justifiably relied on a previous ruling, regulation, or opinion, and a change in IRS policy, rather than a correction of a prior erroneous interpretation of the tax law, would result in increased taxpayer liability.

In the case of the foreign tax credit as utilized by the petroleum companies, the companies were on notice as early as 1973 that the IRS questioned their use of this credit. In that year, IRS stated that certain petroleum company audits were being held in abeyance because of questions concerning the foreign tax credit. In 1976, the IRS went further, and promulgated guidelines which denied the foreign tax credit to oil companies. The tremendous increases in oil prices and the changes in pricing policy which occurred in 1973 so altered the situation that it was clear to all concerned that the 1955 ruling was based on a foreign set of circumstances. Thus, the taxpayers activities were not within the factual parameters of the prior ruling, and the January 1978 ruling was in the nature of a correction of a prior, erroneous IRS action. Either of these would disqualify the petroleum companies from receiving retroactive application of the ruling denying them the use of the foreign tax credit. The law on these points is clear: the IRS did not have the authority to delay its ruling, and it should have applied it retroactively.

Additional Views of Hon. Garry Brown, Hon. Frank Horton, Hon. John N. Erlenborn, Hon. Paul N. McCloskey, Jr., and Thomas N. Kindness

We support this subcommittee report and agree with most of its findings especially where it criticizes attempts by government officials to interfere with IRS decisionmaking on "policy" grounds. In our opinion the IRS rulings and regulations processes on matters of tax administration and should be free from such interference. The duly enacted statutory provisions of the Internal Revenue Code should not be subverted to conform to a "policy" articulated by some unknown person in the executive branch.

However, we disagree with the position that the IRS should have retroactively applied Revenue Ruling 78–63 which revoked Revenue Ruling 55–296. The report argues that the ruling which had the effect of denying creditability for payments to the Saudi Arabian Government, should have been effective for tax years back to at least July 14, 1976, if not all open years. In our opinion the report presents only one side of an arguable and close question on this point. It is our intention to describe briefly the arguments on both sides of the retroactivity question and put forth our own conclusion on the IRS decision not to apply the ruling for years prior to 1978.

Arguments for Retroactivity

The committee report states the arguments for applying Revenue Ruling 78–63 retroactively. . . . First it is argued that the oil companies knew that the posted prices on which their foreign income taxes were calculated bore no relationship to the market prices on which actual receipts are based. It is the responsibility of the taxpayer to demonstrate that its fact situation fits within the parameters of the general ruling. The conclusion is that the oil companies could not have reasonably relied on Revenue Ruling 55-296 after the split in posted prices and market prices, and thereby would not be treated unfairly by a retroactive revocation of that ruling.

The second argument in favor of retroactivity also goes to the question of whether the oil companies could justifiably rely on the 1955 ruling allowing the credits. IRS audits, begun before the 1975 tax year returns were filed, raised the issue of the validity of the foreign tax credits claimed, and thus served as notice to the oil companies.

The third argument cites the issuance of IR-1638, on July 14, 1976, which stated the current IRS position, questioning the creditability of foreign payments in mineral extraction cases. Based on the criteria outlined in the new release, the public was on notice that OPEC country tax arrangement would not qualify as creditable income taxes.

Arguments against Retroactivity

There are four significant points as counterargument, against the retroactivity position. First, the current official IRS policy as set forth in Revenue Procedure 72-1, 1972-1 C.B. 693, is:

> Where Revenue Rulings revoke or modify rulings previously published in the Bulletin the authority of section 7805 (b) of the Code ordinarily is invoked to provide that the new rulings will not be applied retroactively to the extent that the new rulings have adverse tax consequences to taxpayers.

Since Revenue Ruling 55-296 was not previously revoked even though some of the facts and circumstances concerning oil pricing had changed, the policy of Revenue Procedure 72-1 should apply in this case denying retroactivity.

A 1977 report of the Ways and Means Committee task force indicates that the legislative solution of putting a quantitative limitation on foreign tax credits was intended to make it unnecessary for IRS to determine administratively the difference between an income tax and a royalty. It says in part:

> Since it is generally quite difficult to distinguish between royalties and taxes in a case of most foreign operations of U.S. petroleum companies, it is felt necessary to provide for a special limitation on these payments.

Third, after IRS issued Revenue Ruling 76-215 which disallowed credits for payments under the Indonesian production-sharing contracts,

Congress legislatively extended the time period during which the payments would be treated as creditable in order to provide the oil companies with time to renegotiate their contracts in Indonesia. (sec. 1035 of TRA 1976). This is evidence of a congressional policy against applying any new foreign tax credit rulings retroactively.

Finally, the legislative history on the issue of foreign tax credit rules for oil companies strongly supports the application of the doctrine of legislative reenactment to any change in Revenue Ruling 55-296. See for example *Helvering* v. *Winmill* 305 U.S. 79 (1938). There are numerous cases in which the courts have viewed with disfavor the Service's attempts to abandon retroactively long-standing administrative positions to the detriment of the taxpayer. See for example *Vogt* v. *U.S.* 537 F. 2d 405 (Ct. Cl. 1976). In such cases the Court decisions recognize that retroactive revocation of a revenue ruling may be so unfair and unreasonable as to constitute an abuse of the Commissioner's discretion under secion 7805(b).

Conclusion

It is evident to us that there are valid arguments on both sides of the retro-activity question, that reasonable men could differ. In questions such as this one we believe it is reasonable for the Commissioner to exercise his discretionary authority under section 7805(b), thereby applying the revocation of the old ruling prospectively only. There is no reason to comment upon whether there may be unique situation in which a decision not to apply a ruling retroactively would be an abuse of discretion for clearly in this instance, it is not; even the majority views do not suggest this. It seems that a sense of fairness in the tax system should permit taxpayers to rely on IRS rulings without concern for retroactive revocation to their detriment. For this reason we disagree with that conclusion in the report.

Notes

1. "Foreign Tax Credits Claimed by U.S. Petroleum Companies" hearings before the Commerce. Consumer, and Monetary Affairs Subcommittee of the House Government Operations Committee, September 26, 27; October 4; and November 29, 1977, pp. 500-508 (hereinafter referred to as "hearings")).

2. Ibid., pp. 500-514.

3. Ibid. pp. 246-250.

4. Ibid., pp. 466-490.

5. Ibid. pp. 5–8; and Treasury memoranda dated February 28, 1974, from Mr. Alexander to Mr. Hickman (Assistant Secretary for Tax Policy).

6. Hearings, p. 230.

7. Ibid., p. 466.

8. Most companies which will be affected by this ruling have tax years beginning on January 1. Consequently, they will not be affected by the ruling until January 1, 1979.

9. See infra. p. 10.

10. Hearings, pp. 368, 382–393. See also appendix 2 of this report for Assistant Secretary Woodworth's concurrence.

11. Rev. Proc. 72–1 C.B. 693.

12. Hearings, pp. 436–438; 443–449.

13. See pp. 5–6 supra.

14. Ibid., p. 348.

15. Ibid., p. 346.

16. Ibid., pp. 343–345.

17. Ibid., p. 345.

18. Steven P. Hannes, now Attorney-Advisor, Office of International Tax Counsel, Department of the Treasury.

19. Ibid., pp. 4–8; 21–106; 146; 152–153.

20. Cable from U.S. Embassy, Jakarta, to Department of Treasury, dated April 23, 1976; memoranda from C. Fred Bergsten to Anthony M. Solomon and W. Michael Blumenthal dated September 23, 1977, with attachments.

21. Hearings, pp. 4–8; 147.

23. See *Tax Advocates & Analysts* v. *Blumenthal* petition for certiorari filed with the Supreme Court on November 12, 1977.

23. *Tax Advocates & Analysts* v. *Blumenthal*, 930 F. Supp. 927 (D.D.C. 1975).

24. *Tax Advocates & Analysts* v. *Blumenthal*, 434 U.S. —, (February 21, 1978, Docket No. 77–631).

Bibliography

Books and Major Papers

Abir, M. "The Role of Persian Gulf Oil in Middle East and International Conflicts." Mimeographed. 1975.

Adelman, M.A. *The World Petroleum Market*. Baltimore, Md.: Johns Hopkins University Press, 1972.

Adelman, M.A. *Oil, Divestiture and National Security*. New York: Crane, Russack, 1977.

Andrasko, Kenneth. *Alaska Crude: Visions of the Last Frontier*. Boston: Little, Brown, 1977.

Askin, Bradley A., and Kraft, John. *Econometric Dimensions of Energy Demand and Supply*. Lexington, Mass.: Lexington Books, 1976.

Ben-Shahar, Haim. *Oil: Prices and Capital*. Lexington, Mass.: Lexington Books, 1976.

Blair, John M. *The Control of Oil*. New York: Pantheon Books, 1976.

Campbell, Robert W. *Trends in the Soviet Oil and Gas Industry*. Baltimore, Md.: Johns Hopkins University Press, 1976.

Carnesdale, Albert, et al. *Options for U.S. Energy Policy*. San Francisco: Institute for Contemporary Studies, 1977.

Chisolm, Archibald, H.T. *The First Kuwait Oil Concession Agreement: A Record of the Negotiations, 1911-1934*. London: F. Cass, 1975.

Eckbo, Paul L. *The Future of World Oil*. Cambridge, Mass: Ballinger, 1976.

Edmonds, I.G. *Allah's Oil: Mideast Petroleum*. Nashville: T. Nelson, 1976.

Engler, Robert. *The Brotherhood of Oil: Energy Policy and the Public Interest*. Chicago: University of Chicago, 1977.

Exxon Corporation. *OPEC: Questions and Answers*. New York, 1976.

Federal Trade Commission. *Report of the Federal Trade Commission on Foreign Ownership in the Petroleum Industry*. New York: Arno, 1977.

First National City Bank. "Why OPEC's Rocket Will Lose Its Thrust." *FNCB Monthly Review,* June 1975.

Georgesen-Roegen, Nicholas. *Energy and Economic Myths: Institutional and Analytical Economic Essays*. New York: Pergamon, 1976.

Ghadar, Fariborg. *The Evolution of OPEC Strategy*. Lexington, Mass: Lexington Books, 1977.

Grayson, Leslie. *Economics of Energy*. Princeton, N.J.: Darwin Press, 1975.

Hollander, Jack M., ed. *Annual Review of Energy*. Los Angeles, California: Annual Reviews Inc., 1976.

Houthakker, Hendrik S. "The Price Elasticity of Energy Demand." Mimeographed. Committee for Economic Development, December 1973.

Houthakker, Hendrik S. *The World Price of Oil: A Medium-Term Analysys*. Washington, D.C.: American Enterprise Institute for Public Policy Research, 1976.

Hudson, E.A., and Jorgensen, Dale W. *Econometric Studies of U.S. Energy Policy*. Amsterdam: North-Holland, 1976.

Klinghoffer, Arthur J. *The Soviet Union and International Oil Politics*. New York: Columbia University Press, 1977.

Knenne, R.E., et al. "Intermediate-Term Energy Programs to Protect against Crude-Petroleum Import Interruptions." Institute for Defense Analyses, paper, September 1974.

Levy, W. "World Oil Cooperation or International Chaos." *Foreign Affairs*, July 1974.

Levy, W. "Future OPEC Accumulation of Oil Money." Mimeographed. New York, June 1975.

Ligon, Duke R. *Federal Energy Administration: Regulation of Petroleum and Petroleum Products*. New York: Practicing Law Institute, 1977.

Lindberg, Leon N. *The Energy Syndrome: Comparing National Response to the Energy Crisis*. Lexington, Mass: Lexington Books, 1977.

Mangone, Gerald J. *Energy Policies of the World*. New York: Elsevier, 1976.

Mendershausen, Horst. *Coping with the Oil Crisis: French and German Experience*. Baltimore, Md.: Johns Hopkins University Press, 1976.

Meyer, Lorenzo. *Mexico and the United States in the Oil Controversy, 1917-1942*. Austin, Texas: University of Texas Press, 1977.

Miller, Saunders, and Craig, Severance. *The Economics of Nuclear and C al Power*. New York: Praeger, 1976.

Mitchell, Edward J. *Perspectives on U.S. Energy Policy: A Critique of Regulation*. New York: Praeger, 1976.

Morgan Guaranty Trust Company of New York. "Oil, Looking Back and Looking Ahead." *World Financial Markets*, January 21, 1975.

Netschert, Bruce C. *The Future Supply of Oil and Gas: A Study of the Availability of Crude Oil, Natural Gas and Natural Gas Liquids in the U.S. through 1975*. Westport, Conn.: Greenwood, 1977.

OECD *Energy Balances of OECD Countries*. Washington, D.C.: OECD, 1976.

Paust, Jordan J., et al. *The Arab Oil Weapon*. Dobbs Ferry, New York: Oceana, 1977.

Price, David L. *Oil and the Middle East Security*. Beverly Hills, Calif.: Sage, 1977.

Reiche, Diana, ed. *Energy: Demand vs. Supply*. New York: H.W. Wilson 1975.

Report of the Twentieth Century Fund Task Force on United States Energy. *Providing for Energy*. New York: McGraw-Hill, 1977.

Shwadran, Benjamin. *Middles East Oil: Issues and Problems.* Cambridge, Mass: Schenkman, 1977.

Taylor, W.C., and Lindeman, J. *The Creole Petroleum Corporation in Venezuela.* New York: Arno, 1976.

Udovitch, A.L. *The Middle East: Oil, Conflict and Hope.* Lexington, Mass: Lexington Books, 1976.

United Nations. *World Energy Supply, 1956–1959.* Series J, no. 4, New York, 1961.

United Nations. *World Energy Supply, 1960–1963.* Series J, no. 8, New York, 1973.

United Nations. *World Energy Supply, 1968–1971.* Series J, no. 16, New York, 1973.

Walton, Richard J. *The Power of Oil: Economic, Social and Political.* New York: Seabury, 1977.

Wells, Donald A. *Saudi Arabian Development Strategy.* Washington, D.C.: American Enterprise Institute for Public Policy Research, 1976.

Williams, Howard R., and Meyers, Charles J. *Oil and Gas Terms: Annotated Manual of Legal Engineering Tax Words and Phrases.* New York: M. Bender, 1976.

Government Publications

Federal Energy Administration. *Project Independence Blueprint, Final Task Force Report: Natural Gas.* Washington, D.C.: U.S. Government Printing Office, 1974.

U.S. Department of Energy, Energy Information Administration. *Annual Report to Congress, Projections of Energy, Supply and Demand and their Impacts.* Washington, D.C.: U.S. Government Printing Office, 1977.

U.S. Department of Energy, Federal Energy Regulatory Commission. *Natural Gas Survey, Efficiency in the Use of Gas.* Washington, D.C.: U.S. Government Printing Office, June, 1978.

U.S. Department of the Interior. *Energy Perspectives.* Washington, D.C.: U.S. Government Printing Office, 1975.

Periodicals

Brown Book (U.K. Department of Energy)

Business International (Business International Corp.)

Canadian Statistical Review (Canadian Ministry of Industry, Trade, and Commerce)

Data Resources Review (Data Resources, Inc.)
First Chicago World Report (First Chicago Corporation)
International Economic Report of the President
International Finance (Chase Manhattan Bank)
International Petroleum Encyclopedia 1976 (Petroleum Publishing Company)
Minerals & Materials (Bureau of Mines, U.S. Department of the Interior)
Monthly Energy Review (U.S. Federal Energy Administration)
Oil & Gas Journal (Petroleum Publishing Company)
Petroleum Economist (Petroleum Press Bureau)
Quarterly Oil Statistics (OECD)
Survey of Current Business (U.S. Department of Commerce)

Other Sources

Electric Power Outlook to 1985 (Arthur D. Little, Inc.)
Energy: Global Prospects 1985–2000 (MIT Workshop on Alternative Energy Strategies)
1977 National Energy Outlook (U.S. Federal Energy Administration)
Outlook for World Oil into the Twenty-First Century (Petroleum Industry Research Foundation, Inc.)
Problems, Resources, and Necessary Progress in Community Energy Policy 1975–1985 (Commission of the European Communities)
World Energy Outlook (OECD)
World Energy Outlook 1978 (Exxon Corporation)
World Energy Supplies 1950–1974 (U.N. Statistical Papers, Series J, no. 19)
World Energy Supplies 1972–1976 (U.N. Statistical Papers, Series J, no. 21)
World Energy Supply and Demand (Predicasts Study 140)
World Supplies of Primary Energy 1976–1980 (Parra, Ramos, and Parra; published by Energy Economics Information Services Ltd.)
U.S. Long-Term Economic Growth Prospects: Entering a New Era (Joint Economic Committee of U.S. Congress)

Index

About the Author

Arnold E. Safer is an independent consulting economist, specializing in energy. He was vice-president of economics for the Irving Trust Company in New York City from 1973 to 1979.

Formerly professor of economics at Long Island University, he held a National Science Foundation grant, and was a consultant to numerous financial and industrial firms. Prior to that, he served as director of strategic planning for Investors Diversified Services in Minneapolis. He began his business career as a senior economist with the Humble Oil Company, now Exxon USA, after teaching for several years at Rice University.

Dr. Safer is a graduate of Brandeis University and holds master's and doctorate degrees from the University of Rochester.

He is a member of the National Association of Business Economists and is on the board of directors of Americans for Energy Independence. He serves on the Energy Committee of the National Foreign Trade Council and on special advisory groups for the Atomic Industrial Forum and the Scientists' Institute for Public Information. He is chairman of the Petroleum Advisory Committee of the New York Mercantile Exchange. He is an active speaker on energy topics in the business community and is frequently quoted in government and media discussions on energy problems.

Dr. Safer lives in Roslyn, Long Island with his wife and three daughters.